# For Entrepreneurs Only

By
Wilson Harrell

CAREER PRESS
3 Tice Road
P.O. Box 687
Franklin Lakes, NJ 07417
1-800-CAREER-1
201-848-0310 (outside U.S.)
FAX: 201-848-1727

FOR ENTREPRENEURS ONLY
ISBN 1-56414-193-4, $12.99
Cover design by Dean Johnson Design, Inc.
Printed in the U.S.A. by Book-mart Press

To order this title by mail, please include price as noted above, $2.50 handling per order, and $1.00 for each book ordered. Send to: Career Press, Inc., 3 Tice Road, P.O. Box 687, Franklin Lakes, NJ 07417.

Or call toll-free 1-800-CAREER-1 (Canada: 201-848-0310) to order using VISA or MasterCard, or for further information on books from Career Press.

3 2280 00602 7593

**Library of Congress Cataloging-in-Publication Data**

Harrell, Wilson, 1919-
    For entrepreneurs only / by Wilson Harrell.
        p.   cm.
    Includes index.
    ISBN 1-56414-193-4 (pbk.)
    1. New business enterprises--Management.  2. Business planning.
    3. Entrepreneurship.   I. Title.
    HD62.5.H37348   1995
    658.4'21--dc20                                                    95-12825
                                                                          CIP

# Acknowledgments

First and foremost, I must thank Scott DeGarmo, the publisher and editor in chief of *Success* magazine, who decided that there should be a column in each issue of *Success* devoted to entrepreneurship. He asked me to become the author. Scott's enthusiasm for my messages to entrepreneurs became the seedbed from which this book was born. It was his idea to publish as a book all the articles and stories I have written for entrepreneurs.

Second, I must acknowledge Bo Burlingham who, as executive editor of *Inc.* magazine in 1985, encouraged me to begin writing about entrepreneurship. Without enormous support and help from Bo and our mutual friend George Gendron, the editor of *Inc.,* my scribbling would never have seen the light of day. It was through Bo and George that I met Bernie Goldhirsh, the owner of *Inc.,* who, in 1987, made me publisher and forever changed my life.

There are so many others to thank: My agent Jeff Herman and publisher Ron Fry are both entrepreneurs. Their efforts are just more proof that entrepreneurs do it better. Then there's Duncan Anderson, my editor at *Success.*

My wife, Charlene, together with my assistant Jo Rennick, formed an awesome team of trusted critics and advisers.

*For Entrepreneurs Only* is a service mark of the accounting firm Ernst & Young. My thanks to them for allowing me to use it as the name for the book.

My thanks, also, to *Inc.* magazine for permission to reprint "Portrait of a Compulsive Entrepreneur" by Joseph P. Kahn (April 1985) plus other stories originally written by me for *Inc.,* which I have edited for the book.

Finally, my humble thanks to the thousands of entrepreneurs who have shared their lives and experiences with me. Each time I'm with them, I draw new strength and energy and determination to make the world understand—*we are the future.*

# Dedication

*I dedicate this book to the two people who, with love alone, gave new meaning to my life and joy to every day: My wife, Charlene, and my young son Corbett. Also to my adult children, Shaun, Niki, Karen and Marc.*

# Contents

## *Spotting a Deal*

## *Raising Money, Growing Your Dream*

## All God's Dangers

## Raising Entrepreneurs

## Uncle Sam and You

# Portrait of a Compulsive Entrepreneur

For a 43-week run stretching from mid-1983 to April 1984, the best show in the Jacksonville, Florida, broadcast area wasn't on syndicated radio or network television but, strangely enough, in the pages of a magazine devoted to local TV listings. The publication was a free (now defunct) weekly called "Jacksonville Cable TV Magazine," and the 10-month miniseries was an autobiographical column called "By The Way..." written by 65-year-old publisher Wilson L. Harrell.

On the face of it, Harrell's "Publisher's Notebook" was a dubious candidate for media stardom. For one thing, its breathless, first-person prose style often read like a marketing manual crossed with pulp science fiction. For another, the author himself was not a famous personage in his home town. Although legendary in certain marketing circles, not to mention in the archives of Procter & Gamble—a company he once taught the true meaning of the word "gamble"—he was mostly a mystery man to his North Florida neighbors.

What Harrell did have and what enthralled his 86,000 readers week after week was superb material, the raw stuff of myth. Country boy, hobo, war hero, entrepreneur, TV producer, mad marketeer, friend of the famous and scourge of the powerful, Harrell had at his fingertips a hundred stories of improbable triumph and at least as many of inglorious defeat. Once those stories started spilling out of him in print, there was about as much chance of stopping them as there was of the author quietly retiring to a tent by a trout stream. Harrell wrote as he has lived: like a man possessed. It was as if the impulse toward autobiography had been there forever, waiting for any available transmission line.

Take, for example, the column dated Dec. 12, 1983. "Last week I gave you Chapter One of the Toasta-Pizza story," began Harrell.

"To summarize, Art Linkletter and I had joined forces with The Peavy Co.—a large and wealthy flour milling company—to introduce a [frozen] consumer pizza product... We knew that once our test market began that one or more major food companies would "read" our test results. If the results were good, they would proceed to copy the product. In February or March they would be ready to introduce their product at the same time we planned to "roll out" of the test markets. [We had] to devise a strategy which would allow us to survive against our giant competitors who would be waiting with fangs bared and sharpened claws."

Brainstorming a new product, campaigning to bring it to the marketplace, feeling the cold threat of competitors closing fast from behind—all were familiar themes to regular Harrell readers. So was the emphasis on "reads" and perceptions, indispensable tools to a master salesman. Even his old buddy Linkletter, no slouch of a shill himself, calls Harrell "the greatest salesman I've ever met," and the Toasta-Pizza saga would not disprove that. Great salesmen love great challenges, and mass-marketing a piece of pizza you could toast at home was surely one of those. Harrell continued:

"Our plan had to be designed to make major competitors think that we were going to do one thing while in fact we planned to do another. Big companies are predictable and meticulously follow standard marketing rules. To be successful, we had to take advantage of our maneuverability, be prepared to do the unexpected, and dare to be different... Let me add that 'risk-taking' is the term used when you are successful. If you fail, it's called 'stupidity.' "

And if you write it down, it's called confession. For, as Harrell went on to explain, Toasta-Pizza proved to be a marketing miracle and a manufacturing disaster. The campaign mocked conventional wisdom: the November launch, a risky time for any new food product to hit the shelves; the 20-city, nationwide blitz after no test-marketing; the use of independent food brokers to do all the hard selling. Despite these odds, retail enthusiasm for Toasta-Pizza was so great that Harrell's team projected their $10-million investment into a $100-million bonanza. Harrell himself loved every minute of it, especially the accolades he received from stunned competitors.

His moment of glory came and went swiftly, however. Unreported problems at the manufacturing plant delayed product shipments long past the date dictated by scheduled advertising. When the trucks finally did roll, they rolled with 40,000 cases of tiny pizzas so badly mangled that about all a toaster could do for them was burn the evidence. While Linkletter fed his grandchildren Toasta-Pizza on network TV, the company's consumer hotline hit meltdown temperature. By the time the smoke cleared, Harrell said in the column, $9 million of Peavy money and a nice hunk of Harrell capital had followed Toasta-Pizza to the bottom of the freezer.

Such a setback might have daunted—or at least silenced—the typewriter of a lesser man. Not Harrell. Every week his column delivered another tale of personal derring-do. Instead of windy essays on civic issues, he wrote of bribing his way out of Saudi Arabia with a passport full of U.S. money, and of how, in 1976, he blew $1 million in seed money trying to bring to the marketplace a (no kidding) three-pound shrimp. Opposite movie blurbs and recipes for Betty's Coleslaw, he detailed his close friendships with Hollywood notables Linkletter and Dan Blocker, and his establishment of one of the largest and most profitable food brokerage companies ever to service American military bases worldwide.

In the waning weeks of Jacksonville Cable's existence, Harrell even revisited World War II France, where, having been shot down during a suicide run against a Luftwaffe squadron, he was hidden from the Nazis by French Communist Resistance forces. Every day, they buried him alive under their corn crop, his only lifeline a garden hose stuck into his badly charred mouth.

Harrell has visited the outer limits of strategic genius. It happened most dramatically in 1967, four years after he bought (for $30,000) a struggling company making Formula 409, a spray cleaner.

In truth, practically everything about 409 was serendipitous, including the fact that Harrell had first-hand knowledge of the cleaner's popularity—his military customers adored it—even among consumers who never saw any advertising for it. And surely it was good fortune when Harrell ran into a food broker in a Honolulu bar, who first suggested and then helped implement a brilliant strategy for domestic distribution: subcontract the ad work and produce commercials in-house, buy air time market-to-market, at discount rates; hire local personalities with local credibility and give them a piece of the action. Nor did it hurt when Harrell wandered into Art Linkletter's office, hoping to buy his high-profile pitchman's services for 409, and eventually walked out with a check for $85,000 and Linkletter in a 10-percent equity position.

But all that was only the warm-up for what happened next, and what happened next was one part luck to about six parts *chutzpah.* "Procter & Gamble waited until we'd gotten up to around a 5 percent market share," recalls Harrell, "and then they got ready to roll out their own spray cleaner. Cinch, I think it was called. It didn't take a genius to realize that, with their marketing muscle, they could blow us completely out of the water.

"Anyway," Harrell continues, "I knew enough about how big companies like Procter operate to know that once they committed to the Cinch campaign, nothing short of absolute disaster could stop them. I couldn't outspend or outpromote them, so I had to out-think them. And believe me, Procter's got a computer somewhere that's programmed to anticipate everything."

What no computer in Cincinnati could possibly have anticipated were test-market results so skewed in a product's favor that disaster was practically built into the game plan. Harrell scrambled the numbers by taking Cinch's test markets and ordering all Formula 409 shipments to those cities delayed. He also pulled all of 409's supporting advertising and in-store promotions. With no real competition, Cinch became one of the most successful new-product tests in company history, causing Procter to sink millions of dollars and boundless confidence into its national roll out.

Then Harrell dropped the other shoe. On the eve of Cinch's nationwide debut, he flooded the market with secretly manufactured, jumbo-size bottles of 409. Shoppers happily snapped·up four-month supplies of their favorite spray cleaner, leaving Cinch to arrive with much ballyhoo and no customers. Early sales of Cinch were so poor, in fact, that Procter must have been tempted to fire its computer along with the several red-faced executives who soon fell on Cinch's sword. Shortly thereafter, Procter abandoned the product entirely, a sur-render with few precedents in the company's long, take-no-prisoners history.

Chapter two: Harrell sold 409 to Clorox for $7.5 million.

All in all, Harrell's balance sheet looks pretty good. Throw out Toasta-Pizza (Why not? Toaster owners did) and a few other ideas whose time never came, and his marketing hunches seem sound. The business record, moreover, speaks for itself. Whether launching a new venture or scuttling an old one, Harrell always stayed right where he wanted to be, at the center of the action.

Well, almost always. Harrell does have one painful regret in recent times: his failure to make a household cleaner called 4 + 1 into the Formula 409 of the '80s. The product itself was not bad—4 + 1 was a liquid concentrate to which the user added water at home, thereby saving considerable money. The organizational principle may have been brilliant. Harrell wanted to (and did) build a "third wave" company: All manufacturing was subcontracted out, all other functions were decentralized, brokers were drafted to lead the marketing effort. There were no—as in none, zero—regular employees. Linkletter signed on as national spokesman, as well as investing (with ex-"Bonanza" stars Lorne Greene and Michael Landon) in the $1 million tax shelter used to finance the venture. And the product achieved major supermarket penetration, totaling 90 percent nationwide, on the strength of the selling effort, a possible world's record for an item with no test markets in its dossier and a paper company behind it.

Alas, consumers shunned it. Says Linkletter, "For 25 years, I've been associated with products sold on their convenience factor: easier to use, more expensive. Here was a product that was more complicated to use but cheaper. We hoped the times were ripe for it to go, but we made a bad misjudgment."

"If nothing else," avers Harrell, "we set up a company that made the product king, and that's all-important. If the product's king—not management or the board, or the sales force, but the product—then you've accomplished something."

And what else did 4 + 1 accomplish?

"We were the first company in history to go broke without going bankrupt."

## For Entrepreneurs Only

It's very possible that when the book finally closes on him, Wilson Harrell will be appreciated as a man of many subplots. Some will live forever in the annals of marketing lore, others will be hooted out of the back room. Whatever their fate, they deserve to be read as parts of a whole, for it is the whole that makes the story worth reading.

Oh, by the way. For all you Jacksonville Cable readers still wondering what happened, here's the last chapter of the Great French Escape. First, Harrell watches from his stretcher as the underground blows up this bridge, see, and then Patton—that's right, General Patton—sends in a tank to rescue Harrell and his buddy. His buddy is a fellow P-38 pilot, and it turns out that the guy driving the tank just happens to be the pilot's brother, although neither expects to find the other there. Really. They throw their arms around each other and throw Harrell on a Red Cross meat wagon, after which...aw, never mind. Wait for the movie.

**Joseph P. Kahn**

# The Soul of the Entrepreneur

# Chapter 1

# Entrepreneurial Terror

I would like to address a few words to a particular group of readers, to those of you, young and not so young, who are starting your first company. By that act, you have joined a very special organization. Admission is automatic; permission is neither needed nor sought; tenure is indefinite. Welcome to the *Club of Terror*.

I myself have been a member of this club, and have known this terror, for close to 35 years. I can assure you that it is unlike anything you have ever experienced. No longer do you have to be bothered with such ordinary feelings as concern, frustration, or even fear. Those gentle things are the least of your troubles now. You can put them away as a child puts away toys. From now on, you will be in the grip of a human emotion that the good Lord, or more likely His nemesis, created just for entrepreneurs.

Now, I realize that you didn't bargain on this when you started your company. Terror is something that entrepreneurs don't expect, can't escape, and have no way of preparing for. You won't find any college courses on the subject—*Handling Terror 101*, or whatever. Nor are there any on-the-job training programs. To my knowledge, nothing has ever been written about it, and few people even talk about it. The truth is that those of us who have experienced entrepreneurial terror seldom admit to it. As a result, it remains a deep, dark secret.

The terror is so secret, in fact, that each of us thinks he or she is the only one who's ever felt it. That's understandable. After all, an entrepreneur, by definition, is a risk-taker who ain't afraid of nothin'. Right? Phooey. Terror is our constant companion, and it scares the hell out of every one of us. If you don't believe me, try something. The next time you meet a fellow entrepreneur, young or old, big or small, male or female, just ask, "So, how are you coping with terror?" You'll probably get a look of surprise or even shock. But if you gaze deep into the other person's eyes, you'll also see a warm expression of recognition. Your fellow entrepreneur may smile, or grin, or laugh out loud, if the monster's corralled for the time being. Then again, he may cry, depending on the status of his current venture. One thing is for sure, though, he'll know from whence you came.

Let me be clear that by terror I do not mean simply an intense kind of fear. The two are quite different. Fear is the sudden rush of adrenaline let loose when her boyfriend walks in, or when you almost get hit by a drunk driver. It's usually accidental, unexpected and short-lived. Entrepreneurial terror, on the other hand, is self-inflicted. It occurs when you, an otherwise normal person, make a conscious decision that carries you over the threshold of fear into a private world filled with monsters sucking at every morsel of your being. There can be no sleep in this world, just wide-awake nightmares. The terror you feel has its own taste, its own smell, and its own gut-wrenching pain. And it doesn't go away as long as you remain an entrepreneur.

I have often tried to figure out what causes this terror, what breathes life into these monsters in the first place. It's not the money. As any successful entrepreneur will tell you, money is just a by-product of accomplishment, and its loss is, well, one of the risks you take, usually with your eyes open. "Fear of failure" is a better explanation, although the phrase seems awfully inadequate to anyone who has ever felt entrepreneurial terror. It's like saying you hate a guy because he wears white socks. The more I think about it, the more convinced I am that the terror comes from the same thing that leads us to start companies in the first place—some basic, semi-conscious need to make our mark in the world; to leave our footprints in the sands of time. What we really fear, I suspect, is that we might become another member of the herd and pass into oblivion.

Wherever the terror comes from, it is awfully hard to imagine unless you have been through it. I certainly had no idea what lay ahead when I started my first company in 1953, although I had some experience with fear. That experience came as a fighter pilot during World War II, when I was shot down behind enemy lines. There, badly burned, I was picked up by members of the French Underground, who devised a unique and cynical way to hide me from the Germans: They buried me in a cornfield with a hose stuck in my mouth so I could breathe. The first time they buried me, I lay there for four hours—time enough to consider all the bleak possibilities. I figured the Germans would 1) stick a bayonet through the dirt and into me; 2) riddle the hole with bullets; 3) accidentally kick the hose; or, worst of all, 4) turn on the faucet. For 11 days in succession, I was buried. For 11 days I lived with a new and unwanted friend—stark, raving fear.

## Conquering terror

But I also discovered something else during that period, a kind of exhilaration I had never experienced before. Each time the French partisans dug me up, I was amazed at how high I felt. I was elated. I had conquered fear and I knew it. Of course, it helped quite a bit that I was still alive.

When I was repatriated, I believed that I had experienced the ultimate in fear—which was probably true. What I didn't realize, and couldn't possibly imagine, was that I was headed for a career filled with experiences every bit as grueling. In the future, moreover, I would put myself through this torture of my own free will.

The truth began to sink in shortly after I started my first company, a food brokerage representing companies that wanted to sell their products to military bases in Europe and the Near East. Kraft Foods Co. appointed me its representative, and almost immediately sales went out of sight. Everything I did turned into more and more sales for Kraft. I was flying high and making money hand over fist.

# A time for fear

Then one day, when I was visiting the company's executive offices in Chicago, Kraft's president, J. Clyde Loftis, invited me in for a chat. The meeting was great for about 10 minutes, as he heaped praise on me for my selling efforts. The next two minutes weren't so great, as he calmly announced that Kraft was letting its own salespeople take over the military market in Germany—which happened to represent about half of my total commission from sales. He assured me that, naturally, I could continue representing Kraft in the other areas, countries like Saudi Arabia, Turkey and Libya.

I sat there stunned. My income was about to be cut by 50 percent, and my profit by 100 percent. Without Kraft, I was pretty near out of business. My mind was going 90 miles an hour. I could see exactly what had happened. I had sold myself out of a job. I had made it look so easy that some smart aleck had been able to convince Kraft's management its own salespeople could do the work better and cheaper. But maybe Loftis himself had doubts. Taking a deep breath, I said, "Mr. Loftis, if you take over in Germany, I'm going to let you take over everywhere."

He looked at me. I looked at him. Absolute silence. I had, of course, stopped breathing and was in desperate need of a pacemaker. Terror had just joined the meeting. After what seemed an eternity, he said, "Are you sure?" Since I couldn't speak, I just nodded. "We'll let you know," he said.

It took him a month to make up his mind. During every moment of those 30 days and 30 nights, I lived with a terror as vivid and as horrifying as anything I had experienced in the French cornfield. When the letter arrived from Kraft, my hands were shaking so badly I couldn't open it. My secretary read it—and let out a shout: "You did it! You did it!" Kraft had backed down. At that moment, my exhilaration was so overwhelming, the high so intense, that I almost passed out.

Was it worth it? You're damn right it was—a hundred-thousand fold. Thirty years later, my old food-broker company still represented Kraft Inc., not only in Europe, but in the Far East and many other places. What's more, that account became the cornerstone of what eventually grew into the largest military-representative organization in the business. A few years ago, I sold it for more than $4 million.

## The reward for terror

I suppose it was this episode that confirmed me as an entrepreneur and kept me coming back. Aside from the terror, the experience also taught me the second secret of entrepreneurship—its reward. I realized then that the elation you feel more than makes up for the pain you have suffered. That high, like the terror, is an emotion reserved for those of us who start companies. It is food for our spirit—the sustenance that keeps us going from one encounter to the next.

Some people might call this an addiction. I prefer to think of it as a roller-coaster ride. In the beginning, you pull yourself slowly up the first incline, making the tough decisions with a growing sense of excitement and foreboding. When you hit the top, there is a brief, frightening moment of anticipation before all hell breaks loose. Terror takes over as you go screaming into the unknown. For awhile, you feel nothing but incredible fear, interrupted only by a few bumps along the way. Then, suddenly the ride is over, the terror is gone and the exhilaration is all that remains. It's time to buy another ticket. Somehow, though, you know that your first encounter was the worst. You have, to a degree, learned how to handle terror. Thereafter, the intensity diminishes a bit—unless you find a bigger roller coaster.

The important thing, obviously, is to get through that first encounter, as some of you are trying to do right now. Don't be alarmed if it seems to be more than you can stand. Recognize the terror for what it is; and get used to it, because it could be yours for life. Learn to look it squarely in the eye and spit on it. If you don't, you probably won't make the club, at least not this time. Of course, there's no limit to the number of times you can join.

Now I realize that I haven't said a damn thing to help you deal with the terror or make it go away. Unfortunately, I don't have any practical tips to give you. The only technique that I've found useful is to get in my car, all alone, and ride around cursing with every four-letter word in my vocabulary. If, by chance, you don't know many bad words, write me, and I'll send you my list. Then set aside a day or so, because it will take you that long to say all of them.

## Never share terror

But cursing aside, let me offer a couple of pieces of advice. First, never try to share your feelings of terror with a friend. You will only be passing along the stuff of which ulcers are made. The other person, after all, may never have been on the roller coaster and may not be a member of the club. The chances are that he or she won't be able to deal with the feelings you describe. By sharing the terror, moreover, you are, in effect, asking the other person to share the blame in case something goes wrong. That's against the rules of the club. It is conduct unbecoming an entrepreneur. Leave that to the big companies that have a built-in structure for sharing terror. They call it a "committee," or sometimes "the Office of the President."

Above all, don't take terror home with you. No matter how sorely tempted you are, do not under any circumstances share terror with people you love, unless they happen to be partners in your company. It will only make them despondent and maybe even sick. They put up with enough just living around an entrepreneur. Besides, you need the experience.

There is, however, something you can, and should, share with the people you love. I'm talking about the entrepreneurial high. By all means, take that home with you.

Back to my Kraft story for a moment. My wife at the time will always remember that episode, not so much because I was so miserable during the 30 days I was waiting for the reply, but because of what happened afterward. We were living in Frankfurt, Germany, at the time. As soon as I got my love letter from Kraft, I called her with the news and asked her for a date. She accepted. The day of our celebration, I took her to the Frankfurt airport and we boarded a plane to Paris, where I'd made reservations at the most exclusive and outrageously expensive restaurant in Europe. I started the dinner by ordering a 60-year-old bottle of wine, which cost about $500. The *maitre d'* dimmed all the lights and served the wine with great ceremony. I've forgotten how the wine tasted, but I will never forget the way my wife looked at me. The dinner lasted three days. We shared the high.

## You are not alone

You will have your own highs to share once you have conquered your terror. In the meantime, you should at least be aware that you are not alone—far from it. There is a whole gang of us out here living with the same monster. And you can take some comfort in knowing that terror is an integral and necessary part of every new business started by anyone, anywhere, at any time. Which means that, for every company in existence, there is, or was, some poor soul who bore the cross of terror for all of the people who have benefited. Whether the name was Mr. Kraft, Mr. Pillsbury, Mr. Ford or Joe Blow, they all shook hands with the devil and joined the club.

My own belief is that the ability to handle terror, to live with it, is the single most important—and, yes, necessary—ingredient of entrepreneurial success. I also believe that it is the lonely entrepreneur, living with his or her personal terror, who breathes life and excitement into an otherwise dull and mundane world. From that perspective, the *Club of Terror* is a very exclusive one. Welcome.

## Summary

There is no way to prepare for entrepreneurial terror—no college course or training will prepare you for this special hell. But you are not alone, and the rewards are worth it.

## Lesson

Spit on terror.

# The Third Market: Engines of America

During the past two decades, a lot of men and women have learned to live with terror. The result has been an explosion of entrepreneurism in America that has spawned an economic revolution like no other in recorded history. Not here. Not anywhere. The result has been the creation of a whole new economic entity: the "Entrepreneurial Market." I call it the "Third Market." The constituents are unique. They are different in character and mindset from any other segment of the economy. They don't think like CEOs of the "large" corporations; and mentally live in a totally different world from operators of "small" companies. They are a new breed. Our world will never be the same. Amen!

As this Third Market forced its way into the staid and disciplined universe of economics, incredible turmoil was created. The Third Market made the strategic marketing plans for large corporations antiquated before they were created. Most advertising campaigns systematically ignored a major subset of purchasers. Sales programs bypassed the most robust segment of the market. Government ignored the primary creator of jobs. Taxing authorities enacted recessionary laws. The result? Economic chaos. One can make a case that had the Third Market been recognized, if entrepreneurs had been nurtured, not stifled, the Recession would never have been. Sad but true, the scenario goes on.

And, the "growing" goes on. In a recent survey of the members of The Council of Growing Companies, a national organization composed exclusively of Third Market CEOs, 79 percent of those entrepreneurs expect their company to grow 40 percent in sales and 39 percent in personnel during the next two years. That hardly sounds like "recession" or "slow growth," even though the numbers are way down from where they were a few years ago.

## Secret dynamos

It's not surprising that the Third Market has gone unnoticed. The entrepreneurs who run those fast-growing companies are workaholics. Their average work week is 75 to 80 hours. They are, without doubt, the hardest people in America to reach. They don't have time to return calls or spend time chatting with sales people, or listening to the latest jokes. They don't read many magazines; they fire secretaries if junk mail gets through. They watch less television than any other segment of the business world; listen to almost no radio, except news and perhaps Rush Limbaugh. They are nonjoiners, nonvolunteers, nonanything that takes them away from their obsession to grow their companies. Even school plays and Little League games are a rare luxury. Canceled vacations and broken dinner dates are part of their world. Loneliness and stark-raving terror are their constant companions.

## Where are they?

They are not only difficult to find, but even more difficult to *sell*. Entrepreneurs want solutions, not some ding-a-ling salesman trying to sell a box of something to make quota.

All this adds up to a mind-boggling result: *The whole Entrepreneurial Market—all 1 million of us—are excluded from the average marketing plan.* We are simply thrown in with whatever effort is aimed at "small" companies. But as entrepreneurs who run fast-growing companies, we don't think of ourselves as "small." As a matter of fact, research reveals that in mindset, Third Market CEOs are closer to the president of General Motors than they are to the owner of a local pizza parlor. To think of us as "small" is a sure way to continue missing, which is what most large companies have been doing for the last decade. Incidentally, "missing" is a masterpiece of understatement in describing what the government has been doing to us. I've got some great words for that. All unprintable.

If you listen carefully, you can hear the corporate drums begin to beat. A few farsighted executives in organizations like IBM, AT&T, Ernst & Young, Price Waterhouse and Merrill Lynch have already seen the light. Others will follow. Over the next decade, I envision an explosion of activity by Corporate America, aimed at the Third Market. Join me in welcoming them with open arms. But, for those dinosaurs who keep spending all their time, money and effort selling each other, good-bye, and good riddance. Incidentally, that goes for most politicians and the horses they've been riding, too.

## Summary

Entrepreneurs have created a new marketing entity: The Third Market—not "large," not "small," but most emphatically ignored by Corporate America and government. But that will change in the decade ahead.

## Lesson

The big companies that make up Corporate America must make sure their marketing plans include the Third Market, the entrepreneurial companies that give the American economy its life.

# Chapter 3

# The Secret Revolt

The discovery of the Third Market will have a monumental impact on the American economy. The Entrepreneurial Revolution will take its place with all the other economic revolutions. How that market was discovered is an interesting story.

## The Third Market is discovered

When I became publisher of *Inc.* magazine in July of 1987, the marketing staff was in the final process of making arrangements with a large and respected research firm, Yankelovich, Clancy and Shulman, to examine Corporate America specifically to determine how the *Inc.* universe fit into the whole. Among other things, we wanted to know how many fast-growing companies there were, out of the 20 million businesses that file income tax returns each year. We also wanted to know about their buying power.

# Astounding research

When completed, that research revealed some startling facts: There were about 1.4 million companies that were growing at the rate of 15 percent per year or more. The number was surprisingly small, but what astounded me and everybody else was their buying power. By interpreting some numbers, we believed that they were responsible for an incredible 44 percent of the gross national product, business-to-business. In other words, a relatively small group of fast-growing companies, run by entrepreneurs, were buying 44 percent of all the computers, telephones, automobiles and everything businesses buy from each other.

Now we already knew that the large company sector—at that time some 7,500 companies doing more than $100 million in annual sales—were responsible for 48 percent of all business-to-business sales. Of course there was a lot of overlap because some of the 1.4 million were part of the "large-company" sector. But regardless of that, the numbers were startling: Entrepreneurs and large companies were buying 85 percent to 95 percent of all business-to-business products and services. That left between 5 percent and 15 percent to be divided among some 19 million small companies. Incidentally, I should explain, our research was not for editorial purposes. It was intended only to help the sales and marketing staff to better understand our market.

# More astounding research

At about the same time that we were conducting our research at *Inc.*, Dr. David Birch, head of research for MIT and president of Cognetics, had been commissioned by the Department of Commerce to develop some data concerning employment in America. A footnote to that research was the subject for an article written by Dr. Birch for *The Wall Street Journal*, which announced that in the immediate preceding four years, 87 percent of all the new jobs in America had come from just 5 percent of the companies, and that two-thirds of those companies had less than 20 employees.

That research was mind-boggling, but there was some additional information that added a whole new dimension. Over the years, *Inc.*

had asked its readers hundreds of questions about their mindset. There was a clear indication that the entrepreneurs who run fast-growing companies were totally different, in mindset, from the people who run "mom and pop" operations. They also exhibited a different mindset from that of CEOs running Fortune 500 companies. "Size" had nothing to do with it. In other words, entrepreneurs running $500,000 fast-growing companies are very similar to their brothers and sisters running very large fast-growing companies. The common denominator is "fast-growing," not size.

I will never forget. I was in my office late one evening, working on a presentation for the next day. I had carefully outlined the Yankelovich research, and our own interpretation that the purchasing power of 1.4 million fast-growing companies was almost equal to all the large companies in America put together. Next, I quoted David Birch's report that less than 5 percent of American companies had been responsible for 87 percent of all new jobs. Finally, I added our research about the mindset of fast-growing CEOs being totally different from "small" or "large." My closing statement was, "These facts prove, conclusively, that there is today in America a massive new market. A Third Market. And *Inc.* magazine is the only medium reaching that market."

## An entrepreneur finds a niche

As I reread my presentation, I sat back, feeling pretty good about it. Then, suddenly I yelled, "Holy mackerel! What did I say?" It hit me like a ton of bricks. I had said that a Third Market existed. Was that possible? How could a whole new, undiscovered market exist? Where were the economists? Where was Harvard and Stanford and all the professors? Where *was* everybody? The implications left me dumbfounded. It was breathtaking. For *Inc.* magazine, a whole new world would open because we, and only we, had always been "The Magazine for Growing Companies." That's why Bernie Goldhirsh had founded *Inc.* in the first place...to help anyone that was trying to grow his or her company, regardless of size.

As a marketing man, I saw the fast-growing Third Market as a separate and distinct subset of the economy; and it was obviously the market that advertisers must reach. Wow! My mind was going 90 miles an hour. I could already see the future. *Inc.* would become bigger that *Fortune, Forbes* or *Business Week*. I would become the most famous publisher in the history of the magazine business! I went skipping out of my office, with much the same feeling I had when I whipped Procter & Gamble. Little did I know what lay ahead, but I couldn't have cared less. I was an *entrepreneur* with a dream. Getting to the end was just a minor detail.

Later that week, at a speech in Boca Raton, Florida, I announced the discovery of the Third Market and the Entrepreneurial Revolution. I've been announcing it ever since.

## Summary

Research tells us that the Third Market—the Entrepreneurial Market—buys almost half of all business-to-business products and services; creates almost all the new jobs and is different in mindset from "small" and "large." Size is immaterial.

## Lesson

For any company selling a product or service, the Third Market is an enormous untapped and undiscovered marketing opportunity.

# Chapter 4

# Are Entrepreneurs Born or Made?

For the last decade I have wrestled with a very provocative question: Are entrepreneurs born or made? Over and over the question is asked of me when I address entrepreneurs. My answer has been that they are *made*. I go on to say that the quest for freedom, which we inherited from our forefathers, is the motivational force that sparks entrepreneurship. I have never been entirely satisfied with that conclusion, because it left unanswered the undisputed fact that *entrepreneurs* breed *entrepreneurs*. There was also the unexplained reality that most entrepreneurs have inherently different instincts, personalities and characteristics than their fellow man or woman.

Then I met Thom Hartmann and read his book, *Attention Deficit Disorder, A Different Perception*, which boggled my mind—as it will yours. If you are an entrepreneur, particularly if you have children, you must read Thom's book. If you want to know whether you're a born entrepreneur, read the book and find out. It's incredible reading for anyone. Let me give you my synopsis.

# Way back when

At one time the entire human race was made up of "hunters." From pre-caveman, throughout ancient history, our ancestors hunted to live. Then, as time passed and people sought a more secure and stable way of life, farming replaced hunting as the way to put food on the table. From generation to generation, successful farmers replaced hunters until the present, when hunting is only a sport.

But as any geneticist will tell you, genes are difficult to kill...that regardless of time, some basic reclusive genes will manage to survive. In other words the "hunter" genes from our caveman forefathers have been carefully preserved and handed down, in varying degrees, to some of us. So today, in a world totally dominated by *farmers*, there are some *hunters* still running around, trying to hunt for a living. *And there, my friend, is the seedbed from which most entrepreneurs evolve.* If you don't believe me, read on.

# Are you a hunter?

Let me list the dominant characteristics of a hunter. If you are an entrepreneur, see if you don't find yourself as you go down the list:

- Constantly monitoring their environment.
- Able to throw themselves into the chase on a moment's notice.
- Flexible, ready to change strategy quickly.
- Tireless, capable of sustained drives, but only when "hot on the trail."
- Results-oriented, acutely aware of whether the goal is getting closer *now*.
- Visual/concrete thinker, clearly seeing a tangible goal even if there are no words for it.
- Independent.

- Bored by mundane tasks; enjoy new ideas, excitement.
- Willing and able to take risks and face danger.
- No time for niceties when there are decisions to be made!

As I examined that list of characteristics, I saw myself and all the other entrepreneurs I have known. In other words, entrepreneurs are endowed with a big dose of *hunter* genes.

In Thom's book, he also listed the *farmer* traits, which, of course, are opposite of *hunters*—right down the line. He also listed the traits of a person afflicted with Attention Deficit Disorder (ADD), as defined by psychiatrists and psychologists. Here they are:

- Distractible.
- Attention span is short, but can become intensely focused for long periods of time.
- Impatient.
- Poor planners; disorganized and impulsive (make snap decisions).
- Distorted sense of time; unaware of how long it will take to do something.
- Don't convert words into concepts adeptly, and vice versa. May or may not have a reading disability.
- Have difficulty following directions.
- Daydream often.
- Act without considering consequences.
- Lacking in the social graces.

The comparison of traits of individuals with ADD and traits of *hunters* are astoundingly alike, which means, if I'm right, most entre-preneurs could be clinically diagnosed as having Attention Deficit Disorder. All these years I've wondered what was wrong with me. At last I know. I have ADD. Not only that, but I passed these adaptive genes on to my children. They, like me, and most other ADDers, have had problems living in a world of *farmers*—particularly in school.

## Save our children

I know that most entrepreneurs think our school system stinks. Let me add some fuel to the fire. If you are a hunter, with hunter children, let me ask you a question: How does it make you feel to know that there are millions of kids today being medicated with ritalin or some similar drug designed to temporarily convert some, if not most of them, from hunters to farmers? It is obvious that hunter children need hunter-based classrooms. Smaller classes. More experienced-based learning, visual aids and fewer distractions would nurture hidden talents and, often, brilliance in children who are now failing or whose potential is stunted by the anti-hunter systems in our schools.

But back to the "born or made" question. I have always contended that entrepreneurs come from every walk of life. I still believe that without an insatiable desire for freedom, the entrepreneurial bud will never bloom. Let me pose an interesting question: Since so much of our lives are affected by heredity, isn't it perfectly logical that our fore-fathers also passed some of their "freedom" genes down to us? Would that explain why some dyed-in-the-wool farmers end up being incredible entrepreneurs. Then, of course, there's been a lot of blending and melding of genes over countless generations. So, we end up with farmers who have varying degrees of hunter and freedom genes, hunters who are part farmers, and so on. But it is noteworthy that ADD and entrepreneurship flourish in America, yet ADD is rare in Japan—*and so are entrepreneurs.* Could that be because Japan has historically been an agricultural society, with little need to fight for freedom?

To say that Thom Hartmann's book has seriously affected my life is a masterpiece of understatement. When I think of what might have been, I am eternally grateful that somehow I survived. I cringe when I think of the millions of people who may have become criminals, drug addicts and/or failures because they were hunters unable to cope in a world dominated and ruled by farmers. Their self-esteem and self-confidence fatally destroyed by parents, teachers, employers—even friends—who simply didn't understand. I am profoundly humbled when I realize, that there but for the grace of God go I... and a lot of *you.*

For Entrepreneurs Only

## Summary

There is overwhelming evidence that entrepreneurs are *born*, not made; that they are genetically empowered with *hunter* genes handed down through countless generations. The implications are mind-boggling. Just think what it may mean for corporate management to know in advance who may have a natural propensity for entrepreneurship. However, it's disquieting to know that children may be diagnosed as being impaired with a disorder and medicated just because they inherited hunter genes, and must function in a world of farmers.

## Lesson

Entrepreneurs are born—not made—but thirst for freedom is the spark that ignites.

# Chapter 5

# Are You a Buccaneer or a Farmer?

A couple of years ago I was asked to be on Larry King's talk radio show to talk about entrepreneurship. A caller asked me why I had owned so many companies, why I kept selling out, why I couldn't stick to one thing. The answer I gave—which I lived to regret—was that there were two kinds of entrepreneurs:

## Two types of entrepreneurs

First the *buccaneer* type, who loved to unsheathe his sword, go charging onto unknown beaches in undiscovered lands, killing all the Indians, stealing all the gold, raping all the women and just having a hell of a time. But then, I explained, if you would build a country—or a company—you need a different kind of entrepreneur, someone who will cut the trees, build a home, till the soil, and go about making a community. A *farmer*, if you will. There cannot be a successful, large enterprise, without both characters. I went on to say that the reason I have started so many companies, is that I have always been, and will ever be, a buccaneer.

I got a lot of mail. Mostly good, from entrepreneurs; but a couple were not so good. An incensed native American took me to task, and rightly so, about killing Indians. I tried to explain to him that I wasn't talking about killing *real* Indians. He gave me an emotional lesson on early American history, which included some interesting comments about my ancestors.

Then there was a woman respondent, who addressed me: "Dear Mr. Male Chauvinist Buccaneer Pig," etc. I called to apologize, and explain that the use of the word *rape* was symbolic, and that I had never raped anyone on my buccaneer outings. As a matter of fact, I didn't believe she was serious, and in jest said that in the future, I would say "buccaneeress" instead of "buccaneer," and have them chasing men. She added "smart ass" to her other explicit remarks, and also commented on my ancestry.

But regardless of my stupid remarks on Larry King's show, I'm right about there being two kinds of entrepreneurs. Most of us live for the excitement that comes with creating something, then building a team to make it happen. Walking on the edge, or even on water if necessary—that's what turns us on. Peace and tranquility is an unacceptable state of being. But wait: What happens to a company when it "takes off?" What happens when it grows up and becomes fully staffed, when there are vice presidents running all the divisions? What happens to the "wild one," the buccaneer, who cranked the whole thing up?

There are some options: First, he or she makes the transition from buccaneer to farmer and goes on building a company. Entrepreneurs who can do this are the rarest of a rare breed. Some names come to mind: Ford, Kraft, Watson of IBM, Smith of Federal Express, Michael Dell of Dell computers, etc. Unfortunately, most buccaneers can't make that transition. They try and fail. That's sad, because they are "crushed," along with a lot of people who were part of their dream. Fortunately, most of them bleed awhile, get up and fight again. It's hard to kill an entrepreneur. If you don't believe it, ask Steve Jobs.

The final option is for buccaneers to know what they are—and are not. To face up to the fact that they can never be good farmers. They are a lot better off to sell their companies before they lose interest, and get back to having fun—working 80 hours a week, not sleeping, begging for money, fighting with suppliers, hating bankers, etc. They are the unsung heroes of economic America. Yet, most people have never heard of them, and never will.

There's another kind of entrepreneur, a subset of the buccaneer-farmer clan. They know exactly what they want, and when they get "it," they stop. They take that one risk and, if successful, will never again walk on the wild side. They are content to run their company, while living a sane, normal life. Out of 20 million companies who file tax returns in America, this group constitutes about 19 million of them. They are the "small business people"—Main Street USA, the backbone of America. Even their bankers love them. Most own shops or franchises. Long may they live.

## Don't try to fool Mother Nature

It doesn't make any difference which kind of entrepreneur you are. But, it is vitally important that *you* truly know which one you are. This is not easy. I know. I made some terrible mistakes until I got around to admitting what kind of entrepreneur I was.

In 1953, I started a company in England, selling to American military commissaries and post exchanges. It grew like blazes, expanded all over the world. By 1959, sales had reached $100 million. The company was mature. I had vice presidents of everything. I found myself spending most of my working day poring over IBM reports and other administrative "junk." I would get so bored that I'd go wandering down my executive hallway, looking for trouble. If I couldn't find any, I'd create some.

I had a great company, good people—making money hand-over-fist. Why, then, wasn't I happy? Why did I dread going to the office? If my entrepreneurial boat had come in, why couldn't I just sit back and enjoy it? Because I was a *buccaneer* trying to be a *farmer*. I wasn't making the grade. The frustration spread to my personal life. I was eating like a hog and drinking like a fish, staying out all night and generally making a fool of myself. I weighed 260 pounds and had developed high blood pressure. In short, I was a mess.

Then, by luck, my best friend came to Paris and looked me up. He left the next day, but left behind some sobering words: "Wilson, I don't know what's wrong with you but, my friend, you are killing yourself. Besides that, you're no fun to be with."

One week later, I made my president the CEO, moved from Paris to New York, stopped looking at reports and started looking for something to buy. One year later, I bought Formula 409 and went back to being a buccaneer. I sold 409 seven years later.

## Summary

There are two kinds of entrepreneurs—buccaneers and farmers. It's not important which you are, but it's absolutely necessary that *you know* which you are. The transition from buccaneer to farmer is a difficult journey—few entrepreneurs make it.

## Lesson

It's better to be a happy buccaneer than a miserable farmer.

# Chapter 6

# Entrepreneurial Transition

The whole business of buccaneer and farmer is an extremely complicated subject. I didn't realize how complex the subject was until I read a book by Roy Cammarano entitled *Entrepreneurial Transitions*. It should be required reading for every entrepreneur who is running a fast-growing company. The book deals with the problems entrepreneurs face as they travel up the rocky and lonely path from startup to the Fortune 500. The entrepreneurial graveyard is full of tombstones with epitaphs that read: "Here lies the body of an entrepreneur who failed to understand that the genius who starts a company cannot—*will* not—be the same person who runs a large company." It's true, they look like the same person, but that's just what the outside world sees. Inside, the deceased fought and lost battles against insidious and corruptive forces that destroyed their entrepreneurial spirit.

## So few make it

Let's look at some facts: We know that 50 percent of all companies fail by the end of their first anniversary. I'm not sure that research is very meaningful, because there are a jillion reasons why startups fail...the major one being that the company shouldn't have been started in the first place. But what is important for entrepreneurs, is that by the end of the third year, 80 percent of the remaining companies have failed. In other words, only one out of 10 companies make it to the fourth year. Less than half of the survivors go on to become growing companies, and a tiny fraction make it all the way.

*Inc.*'s research tells the same story: Out of the 20 million companies that file tax returns, only 1,460 have sales of $100 million or more. For every 40,000 companies, only one is a Fortune 500. I believe those numbers would change drastically if entrepreneurs had a better understanding of themselves; what they truly want—and what price they're willing to pay for it.

In his book, Roy outlines for us the four transitional phases an entrepreneur must go through. Study these transitions and remember them. I'll be referring to them again and again.

The first category is the "Entrepreneurial Genius." These are the dreamers with an idea, full of excitement, exhilaration, optimism and hope. Like magnets, they draw everyone toward the realization of their dream. It's a great time for entrepreneurs.

Second, the "Benevolent Dictator," who believes completely in himself or herself, controlling every aspect of the business, a suffocating domination of everything and everybody. In this stage, the entrepreneur thinks of himself or herself as a parent teaching the children what to do—and when and how. It's probably the happiest time in an entrepreneur's business life.

Third, the "Disassociated Director." A truly confusing and frustrating time, full of distrust, inconsistencies and erratic mood swings. As the children grow up, they revolt. Entrepreneurs quickly learn the organization is not, cannot and does not want to be dependent on them for every decision. Employees begin to trust their peers more than the entrepreneur. It's the time for "letting go." A time for potential disaster.

Fourth, the "Visionary Leader," characterized by communication, cooperation and collaboration. The entrepreneur's original dream is fulfilled: To create, build and lead a successful, large corporation.

## I've been there

I have been through all four phases, more than once. I thoroughly enjoyed one and two; hated every minute of three; was bored to death in four. I believe phase one and two are the stages on which entrepreneurs play their roles. It's where they live; it's where America is different from the rest of the world. Phase three is nothing other than a test to determine whether an individual is willing to give up the fun of being an entrepreneur, to become a business leader. Most entrepreneurs fail to make it through this transition, finding themselves trapped in the first two phases, destined to repeat them over and over again.

There was a time when my whole being was consumed by the burning desire to become a Visionary Leader, and I suspect that flame would still be burning if I hadn't made it to phase four. But since hindsight is 20/20, let me tell you loud and clear, that all the limousines, yachts, Fifth Avenue penthouses, fashion shows and swank clubs put together don't make up for leading a bunch of race-horses into the fire and brimstone of an entrepreneurial dogfight. There ain't nothing like it.

## Go for it

Does that mean I'm trying to tell you not to grab the brass ring? Absolutely not! I believe every entrepreneur should go as far as they can to fulfill their destiny. To do anything less would mean you weren't an entrepreneur in the first place. What I do want to say is when you get to phase four—and I surely hope you do—you're going to look back and remember the kind of exhilaration that comes only in phases one and two. When you finally get to phase four—when you are poring over IBM reports, negotiating with bankers, sweating out lawsuits by irate stockholders and cramming for the next directors' meeting, you'll yearn for those precious moments when the world revolved around you; back when you were arrogant, irritating, proud, vane, ruthless—and terrorized. Back when you were an entrepreneur.

It doesn't matter two hoots what phase you end up in, but it's absolutely vital that you are where you *want* to be. That you know what you want out of life, or at least *think* you know. Let me forecast that you'll change your mind along the way. However, I do want to warn you about phase three, and comfort you if you decide not to make that transition—or if you try and fail.

When I talked about buccaneers and farmers, I was talking about phase three. The moment of truth for all entrepreneurs. The time to decide whether to "sell out" and go back to being a buccaneer, or make the transition and become a farmer. The word "transition" is inadequate to describe the anguish that comes with having to change your whole personality. To watch the company you breathed life into become a hotbed for intrigue, as "professional managers" insert their sting. It's like the words "letting go." Sounds so simple, but, remember, when you "let go," somebody else takes over. Suddenly the whole organization is in disarray, politicking becomes a way of life, committees are formed, reports created, reams of rules and regulations printed, creative initiatives stifled, numbers more important than people—and on and on.

I know of what I speak. I've suffered through it. And then, when I made it to the other side of the river, the grass was not greener. It wasn't even *grass*. But then I'm not Ross Perot, or Bill Gates, Michael Dell or Debbie Fields. Maybe you will be. I sure hope so, 'cause heaven knows, all those budding entrepreneurs out there need bright and shining stars to guide them through the dark, lonely nights that lay ahead.

## Summary

There are four distinct and different phases in an entrepreneurial life: First, the Genius; second, Benevolent Dictator; third, Disassociated Director; fourth, Visionary Leader. It's absolutely necessary that entrepreneurs know where they are in order to be prepared for the next phase. But beware of phase three—most entrepreneurs don't make it through that potentially disastrous stage.

## Lesson

Phase one and two are duck soup for entrepreneurs. Phase three is a monster. Phase four may not be all that it's cracked up to be.

# Chapter 7

# The Decision-Making Process

Everybody knows that entrepreneurs are decision-makers. We hear a lot about the few who make wise decisions, but not much is written about the failures. And whether we like it or not, that's where most would-be entrepreneurs wind up. After talking to thousands of winners and losers, I'm convinced that it's the *process* of decision-making that determines who will make it through the pearly gates. For an entrepreneur, decision-making is extremely complex, because the *process* must change as we go from startup to running a large organization—as we go through the four entrepreneurial transitions.

During the Genius or startup phase, the *process* is very simple. There *ain't* no process. Questions in....instant answers out. The budding entrepreneur is the source of all knowledge. And that's as it should be because, as we all know, if the *genius* does the unthinkable and asks for advice, he'll only be told he's "nuts" to start in the first place. Unfortunately, this is the phase that any single bad decision, even a small one, will destroy the company—which is what usually happens. I don't really have any advice for entrepreneurs in this stage. Or, let me say it differently: I have some advice, but I know you won't listen.

During the next stage (Benevolent Dictator), the decision-making *process* begins to change—although the entrepreneur has become even more godlike and would prefer no intervention. And why not? His or her decisions have been infallible up until now. However, some new players have joined the game—people like bankers, suppliers, customers, etc., all of whom have a way of forcing their unwanted opinions into the decision-making process. As the business grows, the intervention increases. But make no mistake, the entrepreneur is still calling the shots. It's just that some new ingredients have been added to the process.

During this phase, one mistake can be disastrous, but unlike the Genius phase, when even a little error in judgment could be a killer, now it would most likely take a "big" mistake to do irreparable damage. The only problem is that the stakes have gone up. There's more to lose. If you're in this phase, I do have some advice: Appoint a board of directors with at least one outside entrepreneur who has been where you are. Allow all policy decisions to be made by that board. It is absolutely stupid not to listen to a wise and experienced business friend's advice on major issues. For a brief moment, give your ego a rest. That, my friend, is the way not to make that "big" fatal mistake.

Let's move on to the Disassociated Director phase. The entrepreneur's nightmare. The company has continued to grow. It's become large enough that the entrepreneur has been forced to delegate real authority. The time of "letting go." Vice presidents are all over the place. If the company is to survive this phase, the decision-making process must change radically. The entrepreneur simply doesn't know enough about all the operations to make unilateral decisions. That's why committees were born in the first place and why they have survived, in spite of the hatred they inspire in the minds of all self-respecting entrepreneurs.

At any rate, the executive staff is an indispensable source of information that must be digested during the process of making decisions. Fortunately, the company has now reached the stage where no single bad decision would spell doom. It would take a number of boo-boos to self-destruct...but the stakes have grown by geometric proportions. Entrepreneurs who refuse to change the process of making decisions are about to travel down a road, along which there are a lot of entrepreneurial footprints.

Yes, I do have some advice. Now, a board of directors is not only desirable, it's absolutely necessary. If, for some reason, you don't want a board of directors, then call it a board of advisers. Call it anything, but do not make major policy decisions without the input from other entrepreneurs. Make your meeting formal; allow your executives to make presentations; force yourself to be open-minded; don't railroad important issues. Let the decision-making process have the advantage of all the wisdom you can muster.

Finally you're there. You have arrived at the fourth stage....the Visionary Leader phase. It's obvious that you've employed the right decision-making process. So, my only advice, old buddy, is, keep on going. But there are two places that you should be looking from time to time: over your shoulder...and in the mirror.

## Summary

The *process* of making decisions must change as an entrepreneur goes through the four phases. If you don't change the *process*, you are doomed.

## Lesson

As you grow, adjust the *process* with which you make decisions.

# Chapter 8

# Facing Fire: Leadership and Entrepreneurs

Of all the qualities that go into making an entrepreneur, "leadership" is an essential ingredient. If you've got it, you know; if you don't, *everybody* knows. You can be an ugly, uneducated, sawed-off, mean SOB. And, yet, for some unaccountable reason, people will follow you to hell. On the other hand you can be a tall, handsome, wavy-haired, handshaking, world-class athlete, with an MBA from Harvard, but unable to lead a squad of passionate perverts to a house of ill repute. Being a "leader" does not mean you can be an entrepreneur, but without it you are swimming upstream without a paddle. I have a theory.

I don't think you can be a true leader until you have been *led*. You can't give orders, until you know how to take them. Psychologists claim leadership asserts itself in early life. They're wrong. Think back to your school days. How many of your classmates voted "most likely to succeed" ever amounted to anything? How many "top of class" at West Point ever went on to become great generals? I believe leadership is acquired, not a birthright. "Combat" produces leaders. The willingness to face fire transposes ordinary men into leaders. It matters not whether the bullets are real—or the more insidious weapons of corporate battle. Leadership is the manifestation of courage.

# War and entrepreneurs

A few years after every war, there is an explosion of entrepreneurism. Why? Because a lot of individuals had a unique opportunity to discover courage they didn't know they had. Taking incredible risks and living with terror became *tolerable*. Is it any wonder when they returned home, they became entrepreneurs? That's what happened to me. Let me tell you just one incident that illustrates my point.

It happened toward the end of WW II. I was a combat fighter pilot, flying a P38. My group was giving "close support" to General Patton in his march through France. Our mission was to bomb and strafe enemy positions ahead of his troops. One day, my flight of four planes was ordered to "take out" an airfield about 100 miles behind the German lines. As a Second Lieutenant, I was flying "tail-end charlie"—the last man in line. Now any combat pilot will tell you that the best place to be when you're going on a "run" is first, because you have the element of surprise. By the time the fourth man gets there, all the antiaircraft guns are ready and waiting. So as I went zooming down, my rear end was eating up the seat. It was my 14th mission, 14 times of knowing all about how many "tail-end charlies" were missing in action. I survived again.

As we pulled up, I saw, way off in the distance, what looked like a whole flock of buzzards flying around. Suddenly I realized: "Holy mackerel, those are airplanes and they can't be ours. They are German Fighters." So, I got on the intercom and called in to my leader, Major Jerry Gardner. In a voice about 10 octaves above high "C," I yelled: "Jerry, there are a whole mess of 'bogeys' at 10 o'clock low." Jerry looked, and then calmly said: "Let's go get 'em."

# Fire fight

Off we went, four idiots, chasing what turned out to be 67 enemy fighters. Not just enemy fighters, but the dreaded Hermann Goering Yellow Nose Fighters. Let me explain: Toward the end of the war, America had destroyed most of the Luftwaffe. So Herr General Goering, the head of the German Air Force, brought together his best pilots. Because they always flew together, they were invincible. They'd had a field day bombing our airfields, killing our troops and generally wreaking havoc. They had never been challenged, but we were about to fix that.

As we got closer, we could see that the "yellow noses" had bombs and belly tanks. They were off to bomb some unsuspecting airfield, and not the least bit interested in playing around with four P38s. They headed away from us. We gradually closed the distance. Finally, they turned into us—67 of them, four of us, coming together head on. Closer and closer. Almost in range. I was back to chewing up my seat.

Now, there is one sacred rule in the Air Force: You always keep formation. Never, never, under any condition, do you break formation. Pilots are taught from day one that the only way to survive in air-to-air combat is to stay together, protect each other. *Stay in formation.*

Well, just as we were about to meet that sky full of yellow noses, Jerry got on the horn and yelled some immortal words: "Every man for himself!" It was a hell of a dogfight. We flew right into the middle of their formation. I was lucky. I ended up just behind the general, who was leading the group, and his three wing men. Nobody behind me could shoot at me, for fear of hitting him, which was a major "no-no" for any German who didn't want to face a firing squad. All of which allowed me to shoot down the three wing men, without getting shot at. Then the general and I had ourselves a world-class dogfight. I clobbered his gourd. He probably flew into my fire, because from the beginning I was squeezing ever trigger in the cockpit. Of course, the second the general went down, every yellow nose that wasn't shooting at Jerry and my other two buddies, opened up on me. I was hit. My plane was on fire and so was I.

I bailed out, pulled my ripcord and looked up. My chute was on fire. Now if you want to know how to stir up some real excitement for yourself, go try that out. Fortunately, I was so low that my chute only swung a couple of times before I hit the ground where, badly burned, I was picked up by the French Underground.

That's another story; but 11 days later, near death, I was rescued by a squadron of tanks sent by Patton to get me out of there. Incidentally, on that day, 47 yellow-nose fighters were shot down. You see, when we first started our chase, Jerry called our group, told them where we were and uttered some more immortal words: "Get over here, we got over 50 yellow noses cornered."

P.S. All four of us survived. Why? Why did three pilots willingly follow Jerry into what we knew would be almost certain death? One simple answer: Jerry Gardner was a "leader." I became one.

## Summary

Leadership is an *essential* ingredient for entrepreneurs. Combat, whether in war or on the corporate battlefield, is a prerequisite for learning and testing leadership skills.

## Lesson

You can't be a great leader until you have been led.

# Chapter 9

# Don't Call Me *Small!*

The greatest sin committed by companies trying to market products and services to entrepreneurs is to think of them as "small." Yet, that is exactly what most large companies do when they design marketing strategies aimed at us. As I have said and will say again and again, the difference in mindset between the individuals who own small companies and the entrepreneurs who run growing companies is profound. To put us in the same category, is about the same as thinking that a worm and a rattlesnake have the same father.

## An entrepreneur speaks

Somebody ought to straighten Corporate America out. Since I've been trying to do it for years, I volunteer. Perhaps the best way is to relate an incident that happened at an Inc. 500 conference a few years ago. As you may know the Inc. 500 is a collection of CEOs who run the fastest-growing, privately owned companies in America. As *Inc.*'s publisher, I was chairman of the affair, which brought together the current year's crop, plus alumni and spouses. All together about 1,000 strong.

We had invited a well-known speaker to address the group at a luncheon. During his speech he said, "I know all of you run small companies." He went on to make an inspiring talk. Afterwards, I approached a group of entrepreneurs and asked, "Well, what did you think of his speech?" One of the group turned to me and said, "Wilson, there are three things that really piss me off: First, I don't like anyone making a pass at my wife. Second, I don't like anyone trying to steal my company. And third, I don't like anyone calling me small. If that guy didn't know any better, he shouldn't have been here and you, old buddy, shouldn't have invited him." Now, that is not a short answer to a frivolous question. He was insulted and rightly so.

## What is small?

I've told that story to a lot of executives in large companies, and to their advertising agencies. Invariably, they look at me like I was from a strange planet and ask, "What's the difference between 'small' and 'growing?' " "What's their volume?" "How many employees do they have?" I spend the next hour, trying to explain that the Entrepreneurial Market, or Third Market, companies do not have a *size*; but most assuredly, they have a totally different *mindset*. Different problems and different needs. I am always asked, "How on earth can you tell them apart?" That's a good question. Let me deal with it.

First of all, let's examine how large companies go about defining markets, so they can decide where to put what resources. For eternity they have identified market segments by dollars, or number of employees. Their computers are jam-packed with information dealing with company size. Small companies usually fall between $500,000 and $100 million in sales; 25 employees up to 1,000; etc. So once a company passes an imaginary line, it goes from "small" to "large." That's an oversimplification of the complex business of research, but it all boils down to size.

There is another problem with "big-company" marketing mentality. There is a rule, which must go back to Marco Polo, that says:

80 percent of all business is derived from 20 percent of the customers; therefore, that's where 90 percent of all marketing efforts should be directed. What a bunch of hooey! That rule was buried right alongside "management-by-committee" and "bigger is better." However, it's still breathing. It may be around for a long, long time; because it takes a lot more work to creatively deal with mindset than it does to turn on a computer and "crank" out a lot of antiquated garbage.

Let me see if I can give an example that will bring the difference between "small" and "growing" into perspective: Let's say that a man or woman drives a dry cleaning truck, they work hard, save their money and buy a dry cleaning shop. They go to work at 7 a.m., come home at 7 p.m., kiss the spouse, grab the kids and go off to a Little League game. If you go to the office, you'll see plaques all over the walls: chamber of commerce, Rotary or Kiwanis Club, the local Republicans or Democrats. He or she volunteers for everything: United Way, March of Dimes, a pillar of the community. This individual is a "small" business person. However, such a person is not going to make much of a contribution to the economy. He or she will probably buy one computer, one or two telephones, along with regular office equipment and supplies.

## The entrepreneurial life

Now, let's take the same individual and change the scenario: After acquiring that first shop, he or she says to the spouse: "Dear, we are going to mortgage this home—one more time, borrow money from everyone we can, including your mother, and maybe even your brother. We're going to hock everything we own, because I'm about to buy another dry cleaning shop. And then, we're going to hock those to buy another, and those, to buy a third. Because I'm going to be the biggest dry cleaner in this city, this state, this nation."

You have just been introduced to a "true" American entrepreneur. His or her average workweek is 75 to 85 hours a week. Gone are the school plays and Little League games. In the office, the only plaque you'll see is the Inc. 500 or the Entrepreneur of the Year. This entrepreneur doesn't have time to volunteer for anything. He or she takes home an armload of office work. There is one consuming obsession: "to grow the business."

# For Entrepreneurs Only

I admit it. I'm on a crusade to educate Corporate America. I'd like to ask for your help. The next time one of those "jerks" calls you "small," give him or her an entrepreneurial smile, and a message from me: "Partner, the door's that way."

## Summary

The confusion between "small" and "growing" companies is causing enormous mistakes to be made by marketing executives of large corporations. Billions of dollars are wasted as "wrong messages" are sent to entrepreneurs.

## Lesson

We, as entrepreneurs, have a responsibility to Corporate America and to ourselves to educate others in the business community that the Entrepreneurial Market is not the same as the small business market; that "small" is a stupid description of a "fast-growing" company.

# Chapter 10

# How to Keep Score

As I roam around the country speaking to, for and about entrepreneurs, I meet a lot of "wanna-bes" who ask me how to be a successful entrepreneur. I always ask them the same questions: "What's your motivation?" "What are you after?" "What, in your mind, constitutes success?" Predictably, the answers are almost always the same: "Money!" A few say "power" or "influence." Some are more specific: big homes, yachts, private planes, Mercedes convertibles, travel, etc. I have a profound and startling answer for all of them. I say, "If you've got a job, keep it. If you haven't, go try and get one, 'cause you ain't no entrepreneur." Needless to say, I see a lot of shocked expressions. The obvious next question is, "Why, what'd you mean?" Which brings me to the point of my story.

I believe that most entrepreneurs fail because they're not entrepreneurs in the first place. Entrepreneurs are a very special breed. The gate to their kingdom is well-guarded against the "greedy" and "get-rich-quick" schemes. Many knock, few are admitted. It's true today, everybody wants to be an entrepreneur—from New York taxi drivers to Avon ladies, all saying: "I am an entrepreneur." Maybe they're right. But claiming doesn't make it so! There are very few true entrepreneurs. So, be careful before you quit your job, cash in your IRA or pension and go hang up an entrepreneurial shingle, just because you want to make more money, or be rich and famous.

## Money is just a byproduct

Hear me now! Money is not what entrepreneurship is all about. Nor is power or influence. Those are nothing but measures of success. Just materialistic scorecards. The world is full of scorecards. If you don't believe it, just open any newspaper, turn to the financial section and start reading the "scorecards" for Corporate America. Call any large company, ask them how they're doing. They'll send you their financial scorecard, along with a message from the "powerful" and "influential" chairman or president, who will do a lot of bragging, explaining or excusing their "score." Our whole stupid business universe revolves around money, and it's dead-wrong. Every single one of those powerful and influential chairmen and presidents are nothing but scorekeepers riding on the back of some lonely and terrified entrepreneur that created the company way-back-when. Back when "money" was a byproduct of wanting to do something well.

Let me tell you what being an entrepreneur *is* all about. It's just one word. Such a simple word: *Freedom!* Freedom to get your head above the crowd. Freedom to be your own person. Freedom to have an idea, and to turn that idea into a business, and that business into an empire, if you can. Freedom to seek excellence. Freedom to care about your product or service, your people, your customers. And, if it all works—freedom to tell bankers, "Get thee to Hell."

Of course, if you make it happen, some powerful and influential scorekeeper may end up taking over your company and passing out scorecards. Even worse, you may forget you're an entrepreneur and become just another scorekeeper.

Think about that for a moment. Isn't that scenario exactly what has happened to almost every single supersuccessful entrepreneurial company in America? To Bill Watson at IBM? To Steve Jobs at Apple?

To Bill Gates at Microsoft? To Fred Smith at Federal Express? Didn't every one of them get caught up in Wall Street's scorecard of success—money?

If the answer is yes, and I think it is, there is the more disturbing question of *why*. Why did those incredible entrepreneurs swap freedom for cash? The answer is simple: They needed money to grow their companies. Lots of money. They were forced to forsake all the things that made them great in the first place. Forced to swap freedom for pieces of gold. Forced to start thinking about short-term profits instead of what's right for their product, customers and people. The *future* becomes "next quarter." So begins the death spiral. The end is inevitable. Is it any wonder that the Fortune 500 is disappearing faster than moonshine at a preacher's retreat? Do you believe for one moment that IBM would be going through its crisis today, if it had not lost its entrepreneurial spirit? No way! The most amazing thing is that even the powerful and influential will admit, privately, that it's all wrong.

## Never sell your freedom

But what does all this mean to you and me? Are all entrepreneurs doomed to follow the same sick financial trek? I hope not. I have a dream. A dream that someday this nation will begin to understand that this month's profit—compared to last month's or last year's—is not the way to keep score. That Wall Street is an imperfect and fatally flawed scorekeeper. I have a dream that the time will come when wiser and less greedy analysts will begin to understand that a company's value cannot be reflected in any financial statement; certainly not in daily stock quotations. I dream of the time when companies will be evaluated because of their products and services; their customers; and above all their employees. When management will be scored on its ability to let *freedom* flourish throughout the organization. When every employee will feel free to contribute ideas; free to be an integral part of the company's entrepreneurial spirit. What a day that will be!

That dream may not be as far off as some may think. Even as I speak, investors are beginning to see the light. Let me ask you a simple question: If you had your choice as an investor, would you rather buy into 10 Fortune 500 companies, or into 10 privately owned companies whose founders and CEOs had all been designated Entrepreneur of the Year? Another question: Why are over-the-counter stocks whipping the devil out of stocks on the New York Stock Exchange? Is it because that's the best place to buy into entre-preneurship? You bet!

Is there a lesson in all this for Bill Gates, Michael Dell and all the other entrepreneurs who are running "hot-hot" companies? I think there is: Don't ever swap freedom for money. Don't let the financial community con you into making stupid decisions just so they can make quick, greedy shekels by trading your future for "this quarter's" earnings. If that means growing just a little bit slower, so be it. If it means waiting just a little while before you own the world, then wait.

But I didn't start writing this epistle for the benefit of Bill Gates, Fred Smith or for the rich and powerful. So, before I go, let me ask the most important question of all: *Is there a lesson for you?*

## Summary

Freedom, not money or power or influence, must be the motivating force that inspires entrepreneurs.

## Lesson

Before you start down the entrepreneurial path, be sure that you are not motivated by greed.

# Spotting
# a Deal

# Chapter 11

# Are Entrepreneurs Risk-Takers?

One of my most interesting consulting assignments is to lecture sales and marketing people about the Entrepreneurial Market. During that two-hour session, I ask the audience to tell me the qualifications they believe entrepreneurs must have. On a blackboard, I write their answers—willingness to take risks, hard-working, creative, ambitious, dedicated, confident, people-oriented, demanding, etc.

When the list is complete, I circle "risk" and ask: "How many of you agree that entrepreneurs must be risk-takers?" All the hands go up. Then I tell them, "Isn't it amazing that when we ask entrepreneurs if *they* are risk-takers, the answer is a resounding no! How is that possible?" I ask. "All of you, and the world in general, agree that entrepreneurs are risk-takers, yet entrepreneurs say *they* are not. Can anyone explain that?"

None can, so I expound a theory, which I'd like to share with you: *Entrepreneurs are so sure that whatever project they're currently working on is going to succeed that, in their minds, there is no risk.* The obvious follow-up question is: How? What mental process do entrepreneurs go through to eliminate risk? Well, I think it's simply a question of adding "creativity" to "risk." What's left is aggression—naked aggression. And that's what entrepreneurship is all about.

Any time I'm talking to a budding entrepreneur, I ask: "Do you believe this is a risky deal?" If the answer is anything but a resounding *no*, then my advice is: "Go back to the drawing board; keep adding creativity until risk goes away. If it never goes, pass on the deal, no matter how good it looks." The most amazing thing about risk is how different it appears when we look back. Let me give you an example—another of those entrepreneurial moments I'll never forget.

It was 1955 in New York. I was with Bob Blake, the export manager for Minute Maid, one of the most important clients of Wilson Harrell and Co., a company I had formed just two years before to sell consumer products to military retail outlets. For those of you who are unfamiliar with the military, let me explain that commissaries are like supermarkets; a post exchange—or PX—is like a department store or mass merchandiser.

My company was still new and struggling. Like every other entrepreneur building a company, I was spending every dime I could scrape together to expand. I had managed to hire enough salespeople to call on commissaries and PXs all over Europe and the Middle East. Every payday was a new, creative adventure. Minute Maid had taken an enormous risk in giving my startup company its account, but it had worked. Our business for Minute Maid was booming. My personal relationship with Bob had grown, along with our sales.

On this eventful day, Bob told me he had a small problem to discuss: Minute Maid's agent in Newfoundland wanted to take over the American commissary and PX business in that small market. That was understandable, given the fact that military sales there were about four times the size of civilian sales. It was a peanut market, compared to our overall sales. The name Minute Maid meant a lot to our company. At the time it was one of the hottest companies in America. Also, the commissions weren't bad.

Bob knew the numbers. He knew that the commissions from Newfoundland were about one-tenth of 1 percent of the total. The decision for Bob was a "no-brainer," but for me it was different. You see, I knew that Bob, as export manager, was aggressively building an international market for Minute Maid. I reckoned this would not be the last time the military business would be used to attract foreign agents. Today it was Newfoundland, a "nothing" market; tomorrow, it may have been Germany.

I couldn't let it happen, but I was in a terrible position, because Bob had already told his Newfoundland agent he was terminating my company, effective 30 days hence. It was an entrepreneurial moment of truth. It was "risk time." So, I took a deep breath. "Bob," I said, "I understand your position. From where you sit, it surely makes sense. So go ahead with your plans, but while you're at it, you better tell all your other agents in Europe and the Middle East to take over as well."

Bob looked at me and said nothing, just kept looking. I stared back and said absolutely nothing. Silence reigned. Who would blink? Who would speak first? About six hours later, or so it seemed, Bob said, "Wilson, you know that's not what I had in mind. You know that we don't have agents in most of those places." I nodded and kept quiet. Finally, Bob "blinked" again. "Are you telling me that if I take Newfoundland away, you're going to cancel your whole agreement with Minute Maid? Is that what you're saying?" I just kept staring and nodded.

Bob slowly shook his head in disbelief and said, "Wilson, won't the loss of Minute Maid be very serious for you?" I took another deep breath, counted to 10 and said, "Maybe it will Bob, but then maybe not, because I'm going to get another frozen orange juice and run Minute Maid out of the military business."

You could have heard a pin drop. The tension was electric. Bob shook his head and said, "Wilson, I don't believe it. You are not stupid enough to give up the whole Minute Maid account over something as unimportant as Newfoundland. You must be kidding." I replied, "Well Bob, old buddy, you're about to find out." With that, I got up and started walking, very slowly, toward the door. I was almost there when Bob yelled, "Get back here."

No sweeter words were ever spoken. Before that day, Bob and I had been friends, even drinking buddies. Suddenly, a special ingredient was added to our relationship: mutual respect. My relationship with Minute Maid grew by leaps and bounds. With their help, I introduced frozen orange juice to the German civilian market, and made a lot of shekels. That day with Bob Blake ended up being a big day in my life. When I think back, I shudder at the "risk" I was taking as I headed for his door. But at that moment, I was so sure he'd call me back that I didn't feel the risk. Of course, I do wonder: Would I have actually gone through that door?

## Summary

Entrepreneurs are not risk-takers. They are so sure that whatever deal they are working on will succeed, that they do not perceive risk. "Risk" will disappear if enough creativity is added.

## Lesson

If you think any project you're working on is "risky," don't do it. Just do what entrepreneurs do and keep adding creativity until the risk goes away.

# Chapter 12

# How to Test a Million-Dollar Idea

I get a lot of calls from budding entrepreneurs who are still in the Genius phase. They have an idea for a product or service that will change the world. They ask for advice—if time allows, I try to help. So it was when I received a telephone call a few weeks ago from a young woman who, in partnership with her husband, had just set up a company to sell a new consumer product. She told me a story that I've heard many times, and one that's worth repeating to those of you just beginning your entrepreneurial travels.

## At the beginning

They had started their company, spent their savings and taken a second mortgage on their home. Now they were ready to get their product into mass-merchandising outlets such as Walgreens, K-mart and the like, but didn't know where to begin. I listened to her and began asking questions. "Do you have a marketing plan?" "No," she answered, "but we have a great product, and we know that once people see it, they will buy it." "How do you know that?" I asked. "Did you do some consumer research?" "No, but all our friends told us it was a fantastic idea that would sell like hot cakes." "Is the product ready for market?" I asked. "Oh, sure, that's what we've spent all our money on. We're ready to go, but we're not exactly sure how we should go about getting stores to buy it."

I spent the next half-hour or so telling her some of the things that stood between her and the customer. When I finished, she said, "Why didn't someone tell us all this before we spent our money?" I reminded her there were volumes written about marketing new products. "I know," she said. "I even plowed through a couple of books, but they were obviously written for people who already knew everything about marketing." I realized she was right. I couldn't think of anything I'd seen that might be called "Marketing for the Amateur."

So I thought it might be helpful if I outlined a plan for those of you with new products, but without degrees in marketing. At the very least, I can tell you some things you should find out before you quit your job and sell the old homestead. My plan doesn't take a lot of money, but it does take a lot of ingenuity, shoe power and guts.

Understand is that it's terribly risky to introduce a new product. I doubt even one product in 500 makes it from concept to market; in consumer products, the figure may be as low as one in 1,000. It doesn't matter whether you have a great product, a fantastic idea or something your friends say will sell like hot cakes. The rare product that makes it all the way does so only if it's the answer to a real consumer need. And, even that isn't enough. You need to dot all your "i's," cross all your "t's" and have all the angels in heaven on your side.

It also helps if you have $20 million, which is probably the going price today for a large company to launch a new product. Don't think anything is going to happen just because you will it to, or because you are prepared to pour your life into it. But if you are good enough and lucky enough to make it, the rewards are incredible.

## The real test

Let's start out with your idea. The first thing you need to find out is, will it pass the most important test associated with any new product? I call it the "Well, I'll be damned!" test. For any product to be successful, it must have what marketing people call a unique claim. In other words, potential buyers must say, "Well, I'll be damned!" when they see it for the first time. If they don't, your product is probably headed for the graveyard. Big companies spend millions to find out if consumers think their new-product candidates are unique. But since you don't have millions, and maybe not even thousands, let me suggest a do-it-yourself test.

To conduct this test, you must have a sample of your widget. Don't worry yet about mass production or perfection. If it's too expensive to make the actual product, then a sketch or drawing or even a written description will do. The important thing is to be sure that a prospective consumer can easily understand what your product is and what it's supposed to do.

Now, take your sample to at least 20 people—not to your mother, or your brother, or your best friend, but to people who will be objective and won't say things just to make you happy. If most of them don't say, "Well, I'll be damned!" or "Why didn't I think of that?" stop right there. You still have your job, your savings and your sanity. Go no further—your widget is a dog.

If most of the people you ask say the magic words, you're on the right track. Now ask them, "What would you be willing to pay for this widget if it were on the shelf of a local store?" Insist on a specific price. The next question is multiple choice: If this widget were available at the price you suggest, would you:

1. Buy it for sure.
2. Buy it instead of the widget you now use.
3. Not buy it.

Then continue your questions: "How many times a year would you buy it?" "What are you using now?" "Are you happy with your present product?"

Ask these and any other questions you can think of, along with the age, occupation, income level, marital status and so on, of each person. Keep a careful record of each answer. I can't tell you how important it is to be sure you're getting the right answers, not the ones you want to hear. If you want to be sure about the validity of the answers, ask everyone who gives you a positive response if they would like to invest their money in your widget. If they all say no, or if they hem and haw, they probably lied, and you should know that your widget has fleas.

Now, take all of your questionnaires and *spread* the information. If you don't know how, find some 15-year-old kid with a computer. First, you want to know what you can charge for your widget. To get that answer, go to the "What would you be willing to pay?" question, throw out the top and bottom 10 percent of the answers, and average the rest. That, whether you like it or not, is a rough idea of what the consumer thinks your widget is worth. Let's call it the perceived value.

Now you have to subtract the approximate amount the retail store will want for its markup—around 25 percent if your widget is something you eat, drink or clean your house with; 35 percent if it's a household item or an appliance or something you put on your face, hair or body; 40 percent if it's something that is normally sold in a hardware or specialty store. Because these percentages vary, to get more accurate information you should ask three or four local stores what the standard markup is for your type of product. Then you'll have to subtract roughly 15 percent for what it will cost you to sell it to the store, another 15 percent for advertising, 10 percent for warehousing and transportation, 5 percent for administration, and 5 percent for miscellaneous things like interest and your salary.

Again, all these percentages will vary by product category, so find the most accurate numbers you can. One way is to ask people who are in the widget business to give you a breakdown of their costs. They may tell you to drop dead or hang up on you, but it's worth a try. After you subtract all these numbers, you'll have the amount left for manufacturing and profit, if any. When you compare the number with what you think it will cost to manufacture your widget, you either have a *go* or a *no-go*.

If the signs are *go*, the next thing you need to know is what percentage of the people who buy any kind of widget will buy yours. So go back to your "would-you-buy" question, and take 100 percent of the "for sure's" and 50 percent of the "maybe's." Let's call this answer the intent to purchase. If that total is over 50 percent of all the answers, you have a small fighting chance; 65 percent is OK; 85 percent or over, great. If it's under 50 percent, forget the whole thing. You are *no-go*. Up to now, your only cost has been shoe power, so it costs very little to quit.

## Taking the plunge

If your numbers look good and you are still determined to go ahead, take a deep breath, because it's now going to start costing money, and you are still a long, long way from any income. Regardless of your results, don't be misled into believing that the research you have done is going to ensure the success of your widget. It most definitely will not. What it should have told you is whether your widget belongs in a kennel. If your answers and numbers are really good, however, it is just possible you are on the right track, so you can be cautiously optimistic.

I call the next step the *Rube Goldberg test*. It's a bit makeshift, but it does the job. To get it started, you must have a small quantity of your widgets. It's not time yet to worry about building a factory or buying thousands of units, but it is time to get someone to make some widgets for you. If you can make your own, so much the better. Because of the low quantity, be prepared for the cost per unit to be high, maybe outrageous, but that's not so important at this point. You must, of course, develop packaging for your widget, which means that you need an advertising agency's services, if you can afford it. If you can't, go to a company that sells packaging. Most of them have a design department they make available to their customers. Show them your widget and ask for their creative help in exchange for future business. To do the Rube Goldberg test, you must have enough finished and packaged products to put up a small (or large) display in five or more retail outlets.

Now it's time to put on your selling shoes. Go to independently owned stores in your neighborhood and tell the owners you have developed the world's greatest widget, and ask them if you can put up a display in their store. And don't charge them anything for the product, which should be an incentive for them to cooperate. The price will be the perceived value you came up with earlier. The purpose of all this is to find out how many customers, for every 100 who buy any product like your widget, will buy yours. In other words, you are looking for your percentage share of the total widget market.

This test won't be easy to arrange. First of all, most store owners will think you're nuts. Remember, though, they own their own stores, which means they are entrepreneurs. Of course, you are going to get a lot of "no's," but keep trying. When your Rube Goldberg test is over, you will have a general idea of your market share. Of course, you didn't have any TV or radio or newspaper ads, but your widget was on display, which is almost as good. Anyway, old Rube never claimed this was a Procter & Gamble market test. It also didn't cost $2 million.

Now, just before you leave, ask your friendly store owner to compare your sales with the slowest-selling competitor. If your sales were lower, you are probably out of business. Common sense says that no merchant will buy any thing that sells slower than the slowest moving product. On the other hand, if your widget sells faster than their *fastest*-selling widget, you've probably got a winner. In either case, the moment of truth has arrived. Ask the store owner if, based on your sales, he or she would consider leaving the item in the store. If three out of five say yes, call me and let's celebrate.

The test is over, and you now have enough information to play a what-if game. Before you go back and find the 15-year-old kid with the computer, you must know the total dollar sales for widgets nationally. You can get that information by calling the appropriate national association of widget producers or, if you have one, ask your advertising agency to find out. If all else fails, call some local widget salespeople. They know everything.

Now you can play with the numbers. If, during your test period, there were 100 widgets of all kinds sold in your five outlets, and you sold 10 of them, then you have some reason to believe that if you were national you could sell 10 percent of the total widget market. Of course, if you sold only one, then you would have 1 percent, and so on. By taking the total national sales of all widgets and applying your test percentage, you can determine what your dollar sales could be if your widget were available nationally.

The percentages will work for any size market, including your own home town. To figure potential sales there, all you have to know is its share of the national market, and your local newspaper will gladly tell you that. You can have a lot of fun with the numbers, and you can also get some idea about whether your widget can make it in the market.

Some general rules apply to every product category. For example, if your widget is destined for the supermarkets and your estimated annual national sales are less than $20 million, you have a problem. You probably would not be able to maintain distribution, because your small sales would not warrant space on the supermarket shelves. Besides, 15 percent of $20 million is $3 million, and that's on the low side of what you would need for advertising and promotion. Likewise, 15 percent would be needed to support a national sales organization.

Again, $3 million isn't that much when you consider you must pay the broker and/or representatives between $1 million and $2 million (depending on the product), and you'd need all the rest for your internal sales force. If your widget is a specialty item that can be sold through a K-mart or a department store, the annual sales requirement may be much less, even as little as $3 million or $4 million. But the lower the volume, the higher the commission would have to be to interest a broker or representative, and the less you would have left for all the other requirements, including profits and your salary.

## Checkpoints toward the payoff

You are still a thousand miles from success, but you have evidence that your product does answer a consumer need, and you have a general idea as to the share of market you may expect. If everything looks good, you probably owe it to yourself to take the next step, but not without professional help. You now need someone to design a marketing plan for you that includes a national roll-out. Find someone who has had some experience in marketing products similar to your widget. If you don't know anyone, go to the yellow pages. If you can't find someone in your hometown, go to the nearest big city. If that doesn't work, run an ad in one of the many marketing publications or call up a couple of advertising agencies and ask them to recommend someone. A retired marketing executive from a widget company would be ideal.

When you find the right person, negotiate a firm price. It will probably be far less than you expected. The expert will study your questionnaire and the results of your Rube Goldberg test. With that information, and all the other information available, a professional can tell you how much money will be required for what and when; how slowly you can roll out your product or how fast. By analyzing the competition, he or she can also suggest whether you can go market by market (which is the best of all worlds because you can use the profits from the first market to help pay for the second), and so on. The roll-out plan will also determine the level and types of media for advertising and promotion, and it will establish the neces-sary introductory allowances. With the expert's help, you can prepare a total business plan, including forecasts and financial requirements.

When your marketing and business plans are complete, it's time for another *go* or *no-go* decision. If it's *no-go*, you'll feel terrible, and your savings account won't feel so good either, but you'll still have your job and a place where you can lie down and bleed awhile until the next idea gets you up again. If it's *go*, I pity you and envy you, because the moment of truth is at hand.

Now it's time to raise money. From the beginning of time, entrepreneurs have been faced with money problems, and I predict that you will be no different. But you own 100 percent of a product that has proven that it will sell against competition, and you have some indication of the final results. You also have a marketing plan prepared by a professional and a business plan that clearly shows your charted course, and you can project the kind of profits that can be anticipated. In short, you have done your homework. Maybe not quite as the professional would do it, but you are not asking an investor to take a shot in the dark. Into the clouds, maybe, but total darkness? No.

Start your fund raising as close to home as possible—with yourself. You must be willing to commit everything you own. Ask every family member who is still speaking to you to invest. After all, you're about to found a new dynasty for your children's children's children. If you are not willing to make this kind of commitment, then know with absolute certainty that investors will be hard to find. Although investors are being asked to invest money that they probably don't need, they will expect you to invest everything you own. It won't be easy, and you'll learn some new definitions of the word frustration. But if you are willing to make a total commitment, chances are you will find someone who will fly with you.

If you can't get enough money to go all the way, be content to start the first market. Things get easier and easier as you *prove* the marketing plan. When you have raised the startup money, its time at last to quit your job, sell your house and anything else you own.

Let me leave you with a thought: As you walk down the aisles of a supermarket or department store and see all those products on the shelves, stop a moment and think. At some time, way back when, there was another person, just like you, who was faced with the same situation. The name might have been Heinz, or Procter, or Gamble, or Goodyear. But at some point in time, that person was you. Have fun—I wish you luck.

## Summary

Introducing a new product or service requires entrepreneurial ingenuity, shoe leather, sweat and tears. The less money you have, the more of those ingredients you will need. But regardless, you can never do too much testing.

## Lesson

Don't try to launch a new idea until you've tested the water and know that you'll be offering a unique buying opportunity to your potential customer. Test. Test. Test.

# Chapter 13

# The Best Customers
# in the World

Entrepreneurs running fast-growing companies are without any doubt the best customers on the face of the earth. It boggles my mind that most large companies continue to ignore the largest and most profitable segment of the market. When will they wake up and realize that their very survival demands that they get their proverbial heads out of the sand, or wherever, and start romancing the only customers who can ensure their future? Let me say it again. There are reams of irrefutable evidence to prove that the Entrepreneurial Market is not the same as the "small company market." Yet, large companies keep lumping the two together.

## Overbuying is a way of life

The term "growing" describes a company with unique needs. One of the great concerns for any entrepreneur running a "hot" company is that he or she will be forced to stop growing in order to re-tool. The only way to prevent that disaster is to plan ahead, and that inevitably means overbuying. I have never met an entrepreneur who does not buy a *bigger* computer, a *better* telephone system, *more* office space, or anything else that he or she anticipates needing in the future.

What an incredible opportunity for large, established companies to be part of the entrepreneur's "planning ahead" syndrome! With all their resources, they could and should be aggressive partners with entrepreneurs. What a beneficial relationship that would build. The payback for any large company with that kind of foresight would be enormous.

## Profit seeking

If "profits" are the driving force for all large companies, how can they not see the Entrepreneurial Market as the only market on the face of the earth that does not buy price? Entrepreneurs are trying to solve problems, not buy a cheap box of something. Of course, if there is nothing else to consider, *price* will reign; and *gouging* is a sure way to incite a bidding war. But buying price takes time, and time is an entrepreneur's most critical shortage. In large companies, it's different. They invariably have a specialist who makes buying decisions. Buying price is a way of life. Entrepreneurs don't operate that way.

All this adds up to one very big truth and a strong message to large companies: Doing business with entrepreneurs is more profitable than selling to large companies. The number-one target for these businesses should be the 1.5 million companies that are growing more than 15 percent per year.

## A bull's-eye letter

Some time ago, I had an expanded version of this conversation with Bob Focazio, vice president for AT&T General Business Systems. He enthusiastically bought the idea. His first question: "How do I find them?" I said, "Why not make it simple? Start by asking each of your branch managers to find 100 qualified entrepreneurs in their cities. You can help by giving them back issues of *Inc.* magazine that list the Inc. 500 and 100. Suggest they also check past issues of local papers to find all the candidates for Entrepreneur of the Year. "OK," said Bob, "That sounds easy. Then what do I do?" "Well," I answered, "Why not write each of them a personal letter telling them how you feel?" He did. Here's the letter:

Dear _____,

As one executive to another, let me share some thoughts with you.

For the past two years we have spent a great deal of time researching Corporate America. We were amazed to find that a relatively few "fast-growing" companies run by entrepreneurs have been responsible for practically all of America's economic growth during the past decade. We have identified your company as one of those "sparks."

We want to meet you. Not to sell you a box, or make a pitch, but rather to discuss your future plans and determine whether we can use AT&T's technology and resources to support your growth; to keep ahead of your growth curve; to be sure you will never have to stop and re-tool.

In that regard, I have asked my (title), (name) to call you personally. I hope you will take few minutes to meet with him (her), perhaps over lunch, so that we may become acquainted. As a matter of fact I have asked (first name of AT&T Manager) to give me a quarterly update on you and your company.

On a personal note, let me assure you that our interest in you is real. I sincerely believe that the future of AT&T depends on our ability to interface with you and other entrepreneurs, to understand your unique problems and to react immediately to your specific needs. I commit to you my dedication to those objectives.

Incidentally, I'll be in (city), on (date). We are hosting a Breakfast for Entrepreneurs. Wilson Harrell, the past publisher of *Inc.* magazine, and present columnist for *Success* magazine will be our speaker. You are, of course, most cordially invited.

I look forward to meeting you.

Sincerely,

*Bob Focazio*

Bob Focazio

Bob Focazio is a corporate executive who *sees* the Third Market, and is doing something. He's got the bit between his teeth—and AT&T has some mighty big teeth.

What could happen, if all across this land, large companies began to see the Entrepreneurial Market for what it truly is? What miracles of economic growth our country would have if suddenly a substantial portion of the resources of our large corporations were aimed at entrepreneurs and their special problems. And who would be the beneficiaries? Well, everybody, that's who. Profits would soar, stock prices rise; unemployment decrease; and, lest we forget, entrepreneurs would at last take their rightful place as the Economic Heroes of America.

## Summary

Why can't the marketing geniuses in large companies see that the Third Market is the most profitable segment of the market? Why don't they copy AT&T's effort to reach and sell entrepreneurs?

## Lesson

As entrepreneurs, we should all do whatever we can to educate Corporate America to aim their marketing dollars where the profit potential exists—with us, the Third Market.

# Chapter 14

# Betting on the Right Horses

You don't have to worry about competing with big companies for management talent: They don't have the kind of people you need.

Owners of small companies, I have found, worry far too much about their ability to compete with large companies in hiring sales and management personnel. The truth is, there shouldn't be any competition, because entrepreneurial companies should not even consider hiring the kind of people who are attracted to large companies.

Entrepreneurs need employees who are *racehorses*. We need chargers who can make things happen. We need people who are creative and innovative, and who don't know what it means to say something can't be done. It helps if they are workaholics with an excess of nervous energy, and—even better—if they never sleep. But, above all, they can't be the kind of people who like to follow "proper procedures," or who value security over the thrill of the chase.

# For Entrepreneurs Only

Racehorses are, of course, precisely the kind of employees that drive big companies crazy, and vice versa. Most such people wouldn't be caught dead in a huge, bureaucratic organization. What's more, they don't belong there. I recently attended a seminar where one of the speakers, himself a big-company executive, noted that "large corporations *have* to establish the necessary controls to ensure no individual be allowed to take any action that may cause injury to the company."

He is absolutely right. Large companies have too much at stake to let a herd of racehorses loose in the fields. Given their management philosophy, they need people who are comfortable with rules, regulations and corporate manuals; who will take orders and play by the rules; who thrive in a structured environment. I call them "mules."

If you want to destroy a fast-growing company, just hire a mule driver to manage a bunch of racehorses. I know. I did it once, and I ruined a great company.

The company was Formula 409, Inc. The year was 1970. I had put together a team of racehorses who had run a pretty damn good race. We had taken 409 nationally against incredible odds, and we had beaten the living starch out of Procter & Gamble, Colgate-Palmolive, Bristol-Myers and a host of other consumer-product giants. Now we were making money hand over fist, enjoying every minute of it. After each success, you could hear a lot of whooping and hollering in our company offices. We partied together at every opportunity. The company was hot, and we were happy. But I couldn't leave well enough alone. I became a victim of the entrepreneurial disease.

The symptoms of the disease are familiar to every successful entrepreneur. You build a great company, and you start thinking you're the next General Motors. You can't keep your eyes off the giants with their super organizations and their professional management teams. In my own case, I became so mesmerized by them that I convinced myself to begin a management improvement program for me and the company. I began attending every business seminar that came down the pike. I even enrolled in the Harvard Business School's Advanced Management Program, which turned out to be a wonderfully valuable experience for me, but which did nothing to cure me of my disease. On the contrary, it reinforced my conviction that I needed to change the way I conducted business, to become professional.

So I began hiring consultants to help me improve. One of the consultants was a well-known personnel expert who I retained to evaluate my sales organization. After traveling around the country interviewing my racehorses, he came back and reported; "Wilson, you are lucky to still be in business. Your sales organization is a disaster. Your salesmen are devoid of discipline and don't know the meaning of professionalism. I recommend that we replace all of them." He also advised me to hire, at once, a marketing vice president who would have total authority over all sales and advertising. Convinced as I was of our need to become professional, I agreed, like a jerk, to every suggestion.

With the consultant's help, we recruited the marketing vice president from a Fortune 500 company, at a salary slightly higher than my own, and gave him total responsibility over all my racehorses. After his first sales meeting, he said, "Wilson, I don't know how you did it with that crew of misfits and mavericks." So he and the consultant began replacing the racehorses with big-company mules. I was, of course, unhappy to be losing the people with whom I had worked so well, but I didn't interfere. I believed we needed professional management to continue our growth, and that meant bringing in professional managers. My role was to sit back and delegate and let the professionals do their jobs.

## Growing dinosaur scales

Sure enough, they did. Little by little, my relatively small company began to look, act and smell like a miniature giant. We began to lose our energy, our spontaneity and our creative spark. Whereas, in the past, we had always prided ourselves on our innovative marketing plans, the new plans were not even interesting, let along innovative or original. Nor was there any whooping and hollering in the hallways, mainly because there was never anything to whoop and holler about. I also found to my horror that professional managers don't like bourbon or scotch or even beer. They drink martinis (one only) or a glass of wine—which was okay, I suppose. What was not okay was that Formula 409 began to lose market share.

To listen to the professional managers, all the problems were the fault of our brokerage organization, with which we'd previously enjoyed an excellent relationship. Now, however, it was being blamed for everything that went wrong. The brokers, for their part, began calling me and asking, "Wilson, what has happened? Who are these yo-yos? What the hell has happened to the 409 people?"

We were in serious trouble. Our market position was crumbling. Heaven help us if P&G or Colgate decided to make another run at 409. We no longer had the people or the organization that could respond. Right before my eyes, I could see what I had so carefully created going to hell in a hurry. I would have given anything to have my racehorses back and send the mules off where they belonged. But what could I do? Fire the whole bunch? It was too late for that.

Then I got lucky. Clorox Co. picked that propitious moment to offer me $7 million cash for Formula 409. I grabbed the money and headed for the bank with a grateful sigh or relief.

Looking back, I regret the mistake I made, but I certainly don't blame the professional managers I hired. They were talented people who simply wound up in the wrong company. All of them went on to do great things. The marketing vice president became president of a large consumer-product company. Formula 409's product manager became the European manager of a major international advertising agency. The others did almost as well.

No, the blame was all mine, and I learned my lesson: It's a lot more fun to *compete* with mules than to hire them.

## Summary

Entrepreneurs need racehorses to create and build an organization. As the organization grows into maturity, there is a need for professional managers, and therein lies the risk of destroying everything you've built.

## Lesson

*Mules* cannot pull an entrepreneurial wagon.

# Chapter 15

# International Poker

During the next decade, entrepreneurs will explode into international markets like skyrockets. Not only to sell "made in America" products and services, but to open offices, form joint ventures, build plants, appoint agents and all the other things involved with expanding into new worlds. There will be incredible successes, but, unfortunately, the international marketing highways will be littered with the debris of entrepreneurial dreams. Failures that could have been successes, and would have been, had the entrepreneur been better prepared.

I started my company in Europe and lived there for 10 years. I ended up with offices all over the world. I left more than my share of debris. So, before you buckle on your entrepreneurial sword and cast off for foreign lands, listen to an old buccaneer with a lot of international scars, along with a few trophies. As in: *marks, pounds, pesetas* and *yen*.

First of all: *Them people over there ain't like you and me.* To them, an entrepreneur is stranger than a pink-tailed baboon from outer space. We are an unknown breed. On the other side of the coin, we know little or nothing about *them* or *their* culture, and have no intention of learning. In every sense, we are strangers. And in most languages, "stranger" and "enemy" are the same word.

## A secret weapon for them

We cross the seas with what we consider our most powerful weapon in conquering business deals—our decision-making authority. Yet this is the very ammunition that most often blows up in our own faces and results in our defeat. Because, most often we are negotiating with people who have never made a business decision in their whole life. The fact that he—almost never *she*—knows that you are the decision-maker, gives your counterpart a tremendous advantage. Whatever he says is subject to somebody else's okay. You're ready to shake hands and get going. He's ready to "refer the matter."

In most cases, there will be an interpreter, which he needs like a hole in the head. All the time the interpreter is interpreting, the man across the table is planning his next move. Like a snake, charming a chicken, he feels your vibrations, your anxiousness, your eagerness, your impatience. The smile on his face may not be the smile of friendship—it's more likely the lip-licking smirk of a predator, already tasting his next meal.

## A stitch in time

What you *should* do before your trip abroad is spend time learning about the culture, mores and folkways of the people you're about to deal with—as well as a few key words and phrases of their language. Next, spend a lot of time practicing how to *stop* being an entrepreneur. Purge yourself of aggressiveness, arrogance, hurry-hurry, uncompromising, single-minded, know-it-all, "close-'em-fast," etc. I know that means changing your whole personality. But take my word, those great entrepreneurial attributes are deal-busters "over there."

Another thing—never talk about your "rags-to-riches" history. How you started in the basement, outsmarted everybody and built an

empire. You must understand, that's not possible in th.
come across as a liar, bull-shooter or babbling freak. It,
understate everything. If you must talk about your succ
it was because you had contacts with organized crime, ,rried
well, or your father was very rich. They'll understand that.

You should try to fool them into believing that you are like them.
Leave your purple shirts and loud ties back home. Dress as they dress.
Eat what they eat. Drink what they drink.

## Patience and a stiff spine

Above all, be patient. That's their long suit. I can't tell you the
times I had my head handed to me because of my stupid impatience.
With most foreign executives, negotiating is an art form, and the
willingness to wait is their Rembrandt. The same entrepreneur who
spends months working on one deal back home will pack his or her
bags, plan to visit 10 countries in 10 days and close 10 deals. Be smart.
Go to one country with an open return ticket. That way, they'll never
see you sweat. Go into every meeting knowing that there will be
another. Make sure that it's *you*, who says, "Why don't we think about
this overnight?" Or, "Let me discuss this with my people and get back
to you."

A final bit of advice. If you don't use a big-six accounting firm,
start now. Their local partners have in-depth studies of those markets
and the people in them, particularly the executives you'll need to
meet. You'll know the pecking order before you start trying to peck. In
my case, I always have one of the firm's partners with me at negotiating sessions. Amazing how many doors will suddenly open. A side
benefit is that you'll know, in advance, what tax breaks and/or government financing is available. Cheap money well-spent.

For all you women entrepreneurs, I wish you luck, because you
sure as hell will need it. It's bad enough being an entrepreneur in the
international world, but a women entrepreneur simply cannot *be*, not
in the minds of most foreign executives. They simply don't know what
to do with you. I know. I believe I was the first American company to
appoint a woman as vice president of the Far East. She told me hilari-
ous stories about her experiences in Japan and Korea, along with a
few that I can't print, for fear of stirring up an international incident.

Having said that, let me also tell you it worked. She made my company a lot of money, and herself enough to start a chain of gift shops in Hawaii. Her name is Joan Howes. She lives in Maui. If you're ever over that way, look her up. You'll meet a great entrepreneur.


## Summary

Most entrepreneurs will have a difficult time as they enter the international market. Since entrepreneurship is an American phenomenon and "on-the-spot" decision-making unheard of in most foreign lands, impatient entrepreneurs are at a tremendous disadvantage "over there."

## Lesson

Leave all your entrepreneurial attributes at home when you expand into foreign markets. When in Rome...

# Chapter 16

# Japan Is History

Every time I'm at a gathering of business leaders, I end up in a confrontation. It starts when the conversation turns, as it inevitably does, to Japan and how they are "clobbering" America. I listen to eloquent narration about their efficiency, their manufacturing skills, their work habits, how much their management gets from workers, etc. When I've heard enough, I pipe up with something like: *"If Japan was a "listed" stock, I'd sell it short...based on the price 10 years from now."* Stunned silence.

Then, "You're nuts, 10 years from now, Japan will own the other half of the world." They tell me about the support Japanese companies get from their government; how they work together without fear of antitrust actions; how the "family" unions in Japan allow for cheaper labor. I keep nodding. I've heard it before. Not only in America, but in Japan, Germany, England and most of the civilized world. What they say is true...*today*. But I'm talking about the future.

I sincerely believe that over the next 10 years, Japan will become less and less important in the world of commerce. Oh, they may coast for awhile, but as sure as catfish suck mud, they're trekking headlong to dinosaur land, for one good reason. You see, *Japan doesn't have any entrepreneurs*, and I doubt that they will ever breed any. It's against their culture. And entrepreneurship is one of the few things that *yen* won't buy. Without entrepreneurs, you can't build and sustain an economy...or anything else.

What the Japanese have been doing, and doing very well, is taking our ingenuity; manufacturing it better, then selling it back to us. But unless we are complete idiots, that won't last. As a matter of fact, we are waking up. Most of the Fortune 500—those bastions of non-entrepreneurship—are downsizing, which means they will be subcontracting to entrepreneurs more and more. And woe to the Japanese when they feel the sting that entrepreneurs will plant!

# I saw the enemy...It was "I"

I'll admit I've got a lot of "belly fire" about this subject not aimed at the Japanese; they just saw an opportunity and took it. The real culprits are all those American corporate executives who allowed labor union bosses to steal America's work force from them. They dared let somebody get between management and the people who were producing. Our workers began to look to unions, instead of their companies, for goodies. The rest is history: higher wages, more benefits, fewer hours, etc. All without regard for productivity and quality. We began slapping junk together and forcing it on unsuspecting customers. Then we added another ingredient: Our executives paid themselves humongous salaries and bonuses, with total disregard for achievement.

Who paid the price? The consumers, of course. Who got the business? The Japanese, along with the Germans, Koreans and everybody else who lived by different rules. We've paid a hell of a price for that stupidity, and we're still paying. Particularly the large companies, who are still stricken with the disease their forefathers created. Fortunately for America, the Entrepreneurial Revolution came along and, because it did, the light at the end of the tunnel is shining bright and clear.

# Tomorrow is a new day

If you have any doubt about what I'm saying, let me offer some proof: It is an undeniable fact that a major ingredient in the success of tomorrow's companies will be the "software" that runs corporate engines. Well, let me make a profound observation: If tomorrow morning, we put a wall around America's software—if we decided that no foreign company would be allowed to buy a single piece of the software that had been developed in this country—what would happen? The answer is simple: The rest of world would sink into economic oblivion. I think it's safe to say that 95 percent of the world's software has been created by, guess who? You don't have to guess, you know: entrepreneurs. If you go back to the origin of the ingenuity that created new products and services, you'll find some lonely, terrified entrepreneur. We did all the creating, and then let somebody else—primarily the Japanese—manufacture our ideas better.

# Their day will come

The disease that infected the large company sector of Corporate America is very contagious, and the Japanese have already been infected with an insidious killer strain. They may not have unions as we know them, but what they have may be worse. Their commitment to workers and their families is from cradle to grave; which has been wonderful—up to now. But their work force is aging, and Japanese companies have reserved nothing for paying off that debt. Sooner or later those enormous costs will have to be added to the products they are selling us. Perhaps, the cost of living in Japan today is the first symptom. A cup of coffee in Tokyo costs six bucks.

Does all this mean that America will have no competition? No! Because entrepreneurship is on the rise all over the world. For example, right down the road from Japan, there is a tiny island that's loaded down with entrepreneurs. It's Taiwan. I predict that 20 years from now, they'll have a greater gross national product than Japan.

For inexplicable reasons, the Chinese are born entrepreneurs. Go anywhere in the Far East; look up who's running what and you'll inevitably find a Chinese businessman. Hong Kong is a perfect example—even the English couldn't stamp out entrepreneurship there.

Heaven help us if the Mainland ever sheds its yoke of Communism. It'll flood the world with entrepreneurs.

I'm often criticized for claiming that entrepreneurship is the answer to all business problems; that I am single-sighted. I confess to that sin. I believe, with every morsel of my being, that no business can long survive without *creativity*. And creativity cannot exist without *freedom*. And freedom is just another word for *entrepreneurship*. The inescapable conclusion therefore is: *No business or economy or country can long survive without freedom—and its offspring: entrepreneurship.*

## Summary

No country in the world will, in the long run, be able to compete with America. The reason? Simple—95 percent of the world's supply of entrepreneurs reside in our land; and without entrepreneurs, no economy will long survive.

## Lesson

Bet everything you own on America. Bet everything you possess on entrepreneurship...the other word for *freedom*.

# Raising Money,
# Growing Your Dream

# Chapter 17

# A Unique Way to Raise Money

Recently, after finishing a speech in Richmond, Virginia, I was approached by an entrepreneur with an interesting, but not unique, problem. He needed money to launch a new product for his company. Since all his worldly assets were already hocked to a "no-no" banker, he had contacted several venture capitalists or, in his words, venture *vultures*, who in one way or the other wanted *control*. He asked me if I had any ideas. I asked him if he had tried all his friends and relatives. He answered, "Even my mother-in-law." With that, I knew that he was in a state of entrepreneurial desperation. I've been there—more times than I like to remember. I told him about a couple of ideas that had worked for me.

In the early '80s, someone came to me with two great new products: Both were concentrates, which, when mixed with four parts plain tap water, would make a window cleaner for about one-fourth the cost. There was another product that would make an all-purpose spray cleaner, just like Formula 409, the product I had bought for $30,000, taken national and then sold to Clorox six years later for $7 million. I became convinced that lightning could strike again.

To make a long story short, we developed a unique business plan that would allow us to go national immediately with the two products, *4+1 Glass Cleaner* and *4+1 All-purpose Spray Cleaner*. The only things missing were the necessary working capital, plus about $2 million to buy advertising for the launch. I thought I'd better tackle the advertising problem first.

## Thinking like an entrepreneur

Along my entrepreneurial travels, I had met Michael Landon and Lorne Greene, the popular stars of television's "Bonanza." I had become friends with their manager, who I knew was always on the lookout for business ventures for his clients. I proposed to him that Michael and Lorne put up the $2 million we needed for advertising. In exchange, we would remit to them each month 5 percent of the gross income from all sales of 4+1 until they had received back four times what they put up. Simple, put up $2 million—if everything worked, get back $8 million. If things didn't work out, they could write off 85 percent of their investment—their tax rate at that time. However, the new tax law, starting the next year, would tax the income from 4+1 at 28 percent.

What a deal! Since they'd be getting their income "off the top," they didn't have to get involved in management, or worry about who was spending how much on what. Most important, this was not *debt*. It was a non-recourse investment, with zero impact on our balance sheet. We could therefore establish normal banking arrangements.

Was it an expensive way to raise money? You bet. But on the other hand, the margins on 4+1 were such that we could afford the 5 percent. Incidentally, the same idea, with all kinds of variations, could work for company expansion, buying equipment, paying bills, or any other business needs.

We got the money, and had an incredible roll-out, with over 90 percent of all the supermarkets in the country buying in. But I'm getting ahead of my story. We still needed money for manufacturing and operations.

# Keep on thinking

One of our directors was Joe Heilbrun, a financial guru from New York. I turned the problem over to him. He came up with an ingenious idea: "Why not get a bank to finance 'purchase orders' as well as receivable?" "Joey," I said, "no bank will do that." "Let's try," he insisted. Off we went to his bank. When we unfolded Joey's great idea to the loan officer, he looked at us as though we were worms and muttered, "You guys are nuts," folded his papers, got up and walked out of the room.

Three days later, Joey called to say that we had a luncheon date with the president of the same bank, who came, ate, listened, smiled, said we were nuts and approved the plan.

Here's the way it worked: When we received a purchase order, it went immediately to our outside accountants. They verified accuracy, checked the creditworthiness of the purchaser and attested to our bank that it was a *bona fide* purchase order from a legitimate customer. The bank thereupon advanced 40 percent of the value of the purchase order, which was equal to our cost of production, plus shipping. When the customer was invoiced, we faxed a copy to the bank. At that point we got another 40 percent as part of our normal accounts-receivable financing. When the customer paid, the bank took their 80 percent plus interest and we got the rest, which was our profit. It worked like a dream.

By combining the two ideas, we were able to take both products national, supported by network television, pay all of our bills on time and make a profit. All that, without ever putting up a dime of our own money. I wish I could end the story right there.

We couldn't get the product off the shelf—simply couldn't get customers to buy 4+1. Even though it was every bit as good as competition, at about one-fourth the cost, consumers just wouldn't try it. Our TV commercials were great. Our spokesman, Art Linkletter, was sensational—he was also a partner in the deal. Every time Art and I are together, which is often, we keep asking each other, "Where did we go wrong?" I guess we'll never know. But in case anybody out there ever needs some window cleaner or all-purpose spray, just let me know, 'cause I happen to have just a little bit left. Ah well! Just another entrepreneurial learning experience, another chance to bleed awhile.

## Summary

If you're an entrepreneur and need money (and if you haven't yet, you will), if banks say no (and they will), then it's time to put on your entrepreneurial hat and start being creative.

## Lesson

When things get tough, don't rely on standard procedures to find money.

# Chapter 18

# You *Must* Keep Control

As I've said before, there are about 1.5 million entrepreneurs in America today, running companies that are growing 15 percent per year or more. That's another way of saying that there are about a million entrepreneurs running around, trying to raise money—any way they can: banks, venture capitalists, Wall Street, etc. However, most of you will at one time or another find yourselves trying to convince some individual investor to fund your growth—usually, for a piece of the action. Since I've been there more times than most, I'd like to pass on some thoughts and ideas.

I recently got a call from an entrepreneur, who had found a "niche," grabbed the "brass ring," taken the plunge and started a company. It worked. His product was selling, the margins were great. He was growing like the devil. Everything was wonderful. Except—he was running out of money. He faced the entrepreneurial dilemma of either finding an investor or slowing down his growth. He didn't like either option. He had found an investor who was willing to put up the money, but insisted on *control*. He didn't relish that idea, but on the other hand, if he stopped growing, he was sure some large company would come take his candy.

He asked me, "What do I do?" I told him that he was where every entrepreneur has been—or will be. Wrestling with *control v. growth*. My advice to him, as it has ever been to all entrepreneurs: *Never give up control*. However, *control* is a funny word. It means different things to different folks. There is control and then there is *control*. Let me explain.

## Beware of *hooey*

First of all, let's try to understand the mindset of a typical outside investor. If they have any brains, they don't want to fix what ain't broke; or change what's working; or take away the enthusiasm and dedication of the entrepreneur. What they really want is to *control* the money they are investing and make a big fat profit. The easiest way to do that is to own more than 51 percent of the company. But that's the rub, because then they control everything, including the entrepreneur. Most investors will try and persuade the entrepreneur that they won't exercise the control prerogative; that they'll let the entrepreneur continue running the company. That's a bunch of *hooey*. Others will say that they only want control until they get their money back, or make some predetermined profit. That's more hooey.

In rare instances, an investor will suggest that you become partners, with equal control. That's equal hooey. It just means you get to spend all your time arguing or hiring lawyers. Entrepreneurs become entrepreneurs for one simple reason: to be free. If you give that up, then you stop being an entrepreneur, and to hell with that. So, let's talk about some alternatives.

The best way for an entrepreneur to raise "noncontrol" money is from people they already know. People who trust them, who believe in them and their dream. Incidentally, the more the better. I have learned not to worry too much about owning 51 percent. I just want to make *doubly* sure that nobody else does. If I know and trust the individuals, I may be willing to let a number of them, collectively, own more stock than I do, particularly if I have the right to buy them out.

There is safety—and wisdom—in numbers. If all of them agree that what I am doing is wrong, maybe they're right. It's not a perfect solution, but it's a lot better than having any one person own 51 percent, and becoming my boss.

Another thought: Suppose you absolutely must have additional money to survive, and are forced to seek an outside investor, somebody you don't know. You're flirting with disaster, so be very careful. Do anything, but don't give up control. For example, agree to give up 60, 70 or 80 percent of the profits until the investor has recovered his or her investment, plus a reasonable return. Agree that you won't increase you salary, or put your girlfriend on the payroll, or buy a yacht, or whatever. In other words, agree that all the investor's money will go exclusively to building the business. Agree to those kind of controls, but do everything possible to keep 51 percent of the stock out of the control of any single individual.

## Use intangibles to stay in the saddle

I was once faced with a terrible situation. I was either going to get money quick, or I was going out of business. I found an investor. He was one tough cookie. I negotiated my heart out. But finally, it was give up 51 percent, or else. I agreed, but insisted that the company by-laws be changed so they provided that I, as the minority stockholder, would appoint two directors, and the majority, the investor, would appoint two. Those four directors would appoint a fifth, who was acceptable to all.

The investor owned more stock than I did. So what? He did not have *control*. I reported to the board, which neither one of us controlled. I also negotiated that, as president and CEO, I would have options to purchase enough stock to regain control, based on results, over a period of years. It worked. I ended up back in control. The investor made a lot of money. It wasn't a very attractive deal going in, but it was a lot better than seeing my company go down the drain.

A final thought: The best outside investor is always another successful entrepreneur. He or she's been where you are; knows all about dreaming; understands *control*. Entrepreneurs also make the best directors. Take my word: Next to family, other entrepreneurs are your best shot.

Just remember, percentages don't mean a thing. *Control* means everything. To keep control, you'll have to be clever and creative. So be prepared. If you wait until you need money, you'll pay a very high price. Every entrepreneur should start raising money the day they have an idea, and then keep raising for the rest of their lives. That's what being an entrepreneur is all about. But never, never wake up with the realization that somebody, anybody, can tell you what you're going to do that day. If you do, stop reading. You're not one of us anymore.

## Summary

When it's time to raise money—which is a normal state of being for an entrepreneur—never, *never* agree to give up control.

## Lesson

You can keep control of your company without owning 51 percent. Just make sure no one *else* does.

# Chapter 19

# Selling Through Agents

I have experienced a lot things during my entrepreneurial life. I have ridden some wild and bucking broncos—even tamed a few. I've also had my share of losing. But through it all, when there was doubt, I went back to being what I am: a salesman. I have always believed the best way out of almost any business problem is to *sell* your way out.

There are only three ways to get a company out of a recession: 1) increase margins; 2) cut costs; or 3) increase sales. For all practical purposes, the first solution is not a viable alternative during tough times. But the second is the cat's meow, particularly for large companies. If you don't believe it, just read *The Wall Street Journal,* or ask some of the recently unemployed. Corporate America's most beloved commandment is: "In a recession, thou shall fire and cut, until thee be made whole again." Close plants, merge, consolidate, downsize, restructure, force early retirement, cut travel—particularly for salespeople—cut advertising, cut promotion and, by all means, cut commissions to everyone who's out there trying to sell something. Cut and gut. The *law* of the big company jungle.

A third option is to increase sales. And that, my entrepreneurial friend, is where you come in. You and I know that whatever those big bureaucratic monsters are doing just has to be wrong. So let's look for new, creative ways to increase sales. There is one area in which I may be helpful—dealing with representatives, brokers and agents.

Almost all entrepreneurs use third parties in their sales efforts. You may call them agents or representatives or brokers, but they all get commissions for selling your company's product or service. I know a lot about being a third-party salesman. I've spent most of my life representing somebody else. Let's delve into the mindset of the typical representative/agent/broker.

## The sure edge

First you should know that all representatives are entrepreneurs. Whether they have one employee or 100. And entrepreneurs *love* entrepreneurs. That's your first edge, so use it. Establish a personal relationship with every one of your representatives. That's something they'll never get from the CEOs of the large companies they represent. Next, understand that representatives have two basic problems: how to make payroll—this month, and how to stay alive—next year.

Most successful reps have a few large clients, whose commissions make up most of the monthly income. You can't compete with that. But that agreement between reps and their largest clients can be terminated with 30 days' notice. Their nightmare is to wake up one morning and find that they've just lost one of their "majors." Suddenly, all the others clients are nervous, and so is the entrepreneur owner, who goes back to not sleeping. Another edge for you. How? Simple! Make long-term agreements with your representatives. Is it risky? Not if you jointly agree, in advance, on what is expected.

## Free sales power

The whole business of working through third parties, is about getting your fair share—hopefully *more*. Since you can't compete with dollars, do it with security. As the owner of a rep firm, I'm going to make doubly sure that my organization takes care of any client who is willing to help ensure my tomorrow. And what does it cost you? Zippo! What happens to total sales when your whole representative organization has your company's products on its "must-sell" list? Will you get more than your fair share? Does Jimmy Carter eat boiled peanuts?

One warning. Throughout my career as a representative, I was fired more times than I can count, but seldom for the right reason. You see, large companies employ regional managers to interface with their representative or broker. Some are great—they get promoted. Others are the dregs of Corporate America. You can imagine what it's like for an entrepreneur to get fired, for the wrong reason, by somebody who couldn't carry his bag. Incredibly, there's usually no appeal.

Another great edge for you. Why not assure those entrepreneur representatives that they will never be discharged without a personal and private meeting with you? Will that cement relationships? Will that make you, your company and your products just a little more important to those individual who tote your profits around in their bag? Don't answer. Just go try it. If it doesn't work, call me. I'll send you a bag of boiled peanuts.

## Summary

Entrepreneurs have an incredible advantage over large companies in dealing with third-party sales forces. On the other hand, if you are the third party, you'll have to suffer in dealing with idiots who have no comprehension about interfacing with entrepreneurial organizations.

## Lesson

As an entrepreneur, you have an edge. Since most third-party organizations are run by entrepreneurs, use personal contacts and long-term contracts to overpower competition.

# Chapter 20

# Winning the Advertising Game

For most entrepreneurs, the most misunderstood, misused and underutilized relationship is with their advertising agency. In many cases the budget heading "advertising expense" might just as well be called "mystery expense" or worse still, "rip-off." A lot of CEOs, especially in small companies, believe they're being "had" by their ad agencies. That's sad because, for the most part, agency people are bright, honest, dedicated professionals.

So, why the dilemma? Well, first of all, there is the question of accountability. Most marketing activity delivers a measurable result. Not so with normal advertising. You put up your money—lots of money—but never know for sure if it delivers a return. The second problem is more profound: The average entrepreneur doesn't understand advertising agencies or how to work with them.

It's easy to think of advertising agencies as outsiders who spend most of their time brown-nosing in an effort to get more money for advertising. Since more advertising means less money for the sales force and product promotion, political infighting is assured. Corporate holy wars are waged. No wonder CEOs throw up their hands. But that's not the answer. Advertising is an area that desperately needs the CEO's personal involvement. I know of no greater sin than for an entrepreneur to conclude that because he or she doesn't have any experience in advertising, the answer is to go hire someone who does, and delegate that responsibility. It's OK to let someone run the day-to-day activity, but never, never, let anyone but *you* make key decisions about advertising.

I've been on all sides of the advertising world. I have spent tens of millions of advertising dollars through advertising agencies. I even *owned* one. Then as publisher of *Inc.* magazine, I was involved with hundreds of agencies. So let me try to shed some light on one of the most complex issues of our entrepreneurial world.

First of all, *when* and *why* do you need an advertising agency? *When* is easy: the first day you open shop. *Why* is obvious, because, whatever your product or service, you must tell potential customers why they need whatever you're selling. From calling cards to yellow-page ads to full-blown TV campaigns, you need creative ideas that project your message. That's not a place for amateurs, specifically not you and/or your spouse.

## Seeking a partner

Start out by going to the biggest and best advertising agency in your community that doesn't represent a competitor. *Big* may not mean better, but it's the place to start. Ad agencies don't get big unless they're good. The problem with a one- or two-person shop is that it doesn't have the facilities to support you if your company takes off. Don't let an agency's size intimidate you. Go straight to the top. Owners only. Sell your heart out. Try to convince them you're headed for the Fortune 500. Remember, most ad agency owners are entrepreneurs, and entrepreneurs love entrepreneurs. They understand dreams.

Persuading a large agency to take your account is duck soup if you already have a substantial advertising budget. But let's assume you don't. It's time to get creative. Let me give you an example. Recently, I was a consultant to a small company that had developed a dynamite consumer product. What they didn't have was money. They desperately needed a lot of startup creative work, such as package design, copy and layout for sales kits, etc. If things went well, they would soon need print ads, as well as radio scripts and story boards for TV commercials. Obviously, they needed a fully staffed advertising agency. But, they figured, no money, no agency. Right? Wrong.

We met with the owners of an outstanding agency. They liked the product and the people. When the meeting was over, we had an agency that was willing to bet on the future; to invest their creative talent to accomplish all the in-house work with no up-front cost. A home run. How? Simple. We signed a long-term contract, based on sales. Not only did we get a great agency, but we were assured of special attention. A win-win for everyone. You see, I knew that an ad agency's greatest nightmare is to build an account and then lose it. We swapped money for security.

Moving ahead, let's talk about the account executive (AE) who will be your principal contact with the agency on a day-to-day basis. *Who* you get assigned to your account is vital. If you get the wrong person, there's no way to win. The account executive's job description says that he or she is responsible for coordinating all of your requirements with the appropriate people within the agency. There are a couple of other assignments: 1) Keep your account; and 2) Increase your ad budget. This job is political, both with you and with the people at the agency. It's important you get the best AE the agency has to offer.

A word to the wise: Don't try to get any of the top dogs. Agencies are like any other company—their top management is snowed under. That means you won't get the time you need when you need it. On the other hand, if they try to palm off some "junior" or the owner's brother-in-law, give them your old tried-and-true CEO "silent stare" until they try again. What you want is someone who is bright, who knows the agency well, and who isn't loaded down with 50 other accounts. Keep staring until they produce someone who gives you a warm feeling.

Once you're satisfied, help your account executive to be a better politician within your company. The more they know about you and your key players, the better they will function. Encourage your senior executives to spend time with the AE.

Now, for the creative department. You'll have no trouble recognizing them, because they seldom look normal. Don't act surprised to meet some strange-looking individual, with hair down to his waist (if it's a man), or a crew cut (if it's a woman). If they remotely resemble someone you would hire, the chances are you've got the wrong person. Expect them to treat you like a worm—they don't understand brown-nosing very well. Don't get upset when they laugh at your ideas.

If the agency tries to keep the creative people hidden, insist on meeting them: First, because it will make your day, but more importantly, because they are one of the major reasons you hired the agency in the first place. Let the creative people show you their work, face-to-face. What you are looking for is something that is fresh and different, even outrageous. Contrary to the advice you may have received, you are not looking for practical or solid creative ideas. What you are looking for are new and exciting ideas that stir the imagination. What you don't want are warmed-over copies of past efforts—or even worse, something that was designed to please you, and wouldn't sell grits in Georgia.

## Beat the commissions

Now that you know what to expect from the main characters, let's talk about financial arrangements. The principal source of income for agencies is the 15-percent commission they receive for placing clients' advertising in magazines, newspapers, TV, radio, billboards, and so forth. The system has been going on since Moses was a boy, and it made sense back when only ad agencies bought media space or time. But that was long ago. Today, there are media-buying firms that buy hundreds of millions of dollars in advertising. By combining the buying power of a number of accounts, and by making long-term buying arrangements, the media-buying services can offer substantial savings.

While there are agencies, particularly the very large ones, that still make their own media buys, others find it more economical and more efficient to leave purchasing up to media-buying companies. Since agencies can pass the job of placing advertising along to some-one who will probably do it better and cheaper, does it make sense to pay them 15 percent on those billings?

I have another problem with that method of compensation. If commissions are the principal source of the agency's income, doesn't that engender a conflict of interest about how much advertising to buy? Will you be denied new and fresh creative ideas, because it's more profitable for the agency to use the same ad or commercial over and over again? The system is antiquated, and I, for one, think it's wrong. At the very least, it sows the seeds of mistrust.

There is a better, simpler way. Agree with your agency that all advertising will be billed to you at their net cost, no commissions. Instead, you agree to pay them for services performed by the job, or hour...the same way you pay for most professional services. By all means, let them make a profit on your account—even give them an incentive kicker based on sales results! I'm not suggesting that you try to save money, but rather that you try to get more bang for your bucks.

Another idea: Tell your agency to authorize its media-buying service or department to make "opportunistic" media buys on your behalf. You can limit authority, based on dollars, seasonal, and/or demographics. There are times when TV and radio stations, along with other media, are unable to sell a particular spot or space, or they may have last-minute cancellations. Like every other business with excess inventory, they want to get rid of it and are willing to deal. You'll be shocked at the buys that can be made.

As an example, a few years ago, when my own agency was taking a client's product nationally, our media-buying company, Western Media International, was able to get a prime-time spot on a major network for $40,000. The spot normally sold for more than $200,000, but there had been a last-minute cancellation. Such fantastic buys won't happen often, but they will happen, and you'll want your media buyer to be right there when spots open up.

My final and probably most important point—your personal relationship with the top management of the agency. You need their involvement and they need yours, but that does not mean you have to live together. There will be a few times each year when you'll want to sit with them, usually when you are in the planning stage of a new campaign. That's when you really need their professional input. Have an understanding, right from the start, that you'll not ask for many of these sessions; but when it's your turn, you want their full and undivided attention.

So, stop being frustrated about advertising. Get involved. Work out a fair financial arrangement that pays your agency for its services; give them a retainer if necessary; pay them more if they produce. Set specific goals to which they agree. Be sure you have the right account executive. Let the creative people have their heads, and be willing to make long-term commitments.

Advertising is in your budget as an *expense*. Change it to *profit*.

## Summary

Advertising is the most misunderstood activity in the entrepreneurial world. If managed properly, it can turn *expense* into *profit*.

## Lesson

Don't settle for less than the best advertising agency. Be creative in making financial arrangements.

# Chapter 21

# Public Relations: A Secret Weapon

I recently had a dinner meeting with an important new friend, Michael Owen Schwager, one of the brightest of the bright in the world of public relations. Mike is CEO of The Media Relations Group in Manhattan. We met to discuss his plans for a PR campaign for this book. I was mesmerized by Mike and elated with his plans. When the dinner was over, I had that ecstatic feeling that entrepreneurs get when they know that everything is "just right."

After the meeting, I found myself thinking, "I wish every entrepreneur in America could have been with me at that meeting... to see, firsthand, how important PR can be in marketing any product or service." From personal experience, and talking to hundreds of entrepreneurs, I know how often we get so caught up in sales and advertising that we ignore the most effective and least expensive of all communication vehicles.

Which is not only sad, but stupid. If I could relive my marketing life, I would never begin a business, or deploy a new idea, product or service, without retaining a professional PR firm like Mike Schwager's. As a matter of fact, I would retain them before I hired my first vice president, lawyer or accountant. From day one, I would have someone devoted to getting "free" publicity for whatever I was trying to do. Let me give you an example of what the Michael Schwagers of this world can do:

# Happy birthday pizza

It was in 1969. Art Linkletter and I had become involved—both financially and emotionally—in marketing *Toasta-Pizza*, introduced to you previously in this book. After incredible test-marketing results, we were ready to roll out nationally. By then, I had learned the value of PR, and retained a small but brilliant PR firm. One day, just as our roll-out was about to begin, the two partners came dancing into my office unannounced—full of fire and vinegar. With bouncing excitement, they told me their idea: "We want to proclaim to the world that this year (1969) is the 100th anniversary of pizza." I asked a logical question: "So what?" Twenty minutes later, after they unfolded their plot, I sat at my desk—dumbfounded—while it began to sink in. Then I jumped up and yelled, "Let's do it!" And started dancing with them.

Their plan was to contact every TV talk show in America, and volunteer to appear on their programs to celebrate the *100th Anniversary of Pizza*, to talk about its origin and progress down through history until today, when a brand-new innovation would thrust pizza into every household in the world that had a toaster. Of course, when they appeared on the show, they would have a home toaster and demonstrate how easy it was to produce instant Toasta-Pizza, which everyone present would gobble up.

The idea became a plan, the plan became an outrageous PR campaign. It worked like magic. They hired a beautiful young woman, Italian of course, with the gift of gab and a sexy accent. She traveled the country appearing on TV and radio programs, telling all about the history of pizza, while she sold the hell out of Toasta-Pizza. As part of the campaign, the PR firm wrote news releases and stories, which newspapers and magazines picked up and ran all over the country.

All the PR activity was carefully planned to coincide with the efforts of our sales force. It was an entrepreneurial marketing coup, *par excellence*. Every supermarket buyer in America must have seen or heard or read about Toasta-Pizza, because we got a 95-percent supermarket acceptance on the first roll. *Voilà!* That one idea was worth more than all the millions we spent on advertising... at about one-hundredth the cost.

Incidentally, you will probably not be surprised to hear that neither I nor my PR firm, nor anybody else on this planet had any earthly idea when pizza was first concocted and began its march through history. But as of now, we all know, don't we? It was 1869.

If only I could end the story there. Alas, back at the Toasta-Pizza plant, there was this belt that carried the product through massive ovens. The intense heat caused the damn belt to stretch. Not much. Just a couple of inches. Just enough to dump pizza sauce, and all the other ingredients, everywhere except where it belonged. What a mess. A few million dollars later, we withdrew. Another entrepreneurial dream down the drain. But back to PR.

I could go on and on with examples of how PR can accomplish amazing results. But the important thing is for you to realize that PR is a secret weapon that you should use—whatever you're trying to do.

How do you go about it? Well, let me tell you how I did it: When this book was about half-finished, I called my friend Harvey Mackay, the author of best sellers *Swim With the Sharks Without Being Eaten Alive*, *Beware the Naked Man Who Offers You His Shirt* and *Shark-proof: Get the Job You Want, Keep the Job You Love... In Today's Frenzied Job Market*. In my opinion, those books had the best PR I had ever witnessed. When I asked Harvey who had handled his PR, he referred me to Michael Owen Schwager. He also said that on a scale of one to 10, Mike was a 12.

I had a meeting with Schwager—immediately got that warm feeling—and asked for a list of his clients, who I called and got the same answer: "A 12." I had found my man. As to the future, well, we'll see. So will you—I hope. Because, one of the things Mike has planned for me is a 10-city media tour. So, if you saw, heard or read about *For Entrepreneurs Only*, then you'll know from whence it came.

To find *your* Mike, I recommend that you do as I did. Find out which PR firms handled public relations for other successful products or services like yours. Meet with representatives from these firms. Examine their work—in detail. Look for proven results. Finally, talk to their other clients. Keep looking until you get that entrepreneurial warm feeling; then let them become a part of your game plan.

## Summary

Public Relations is an incredible marketing tool. The cost is a pittance compared to buying media. Unfortunately, most entrepreneurs don't start using PR early enough.

## Lesson

Pick a professional PR firm to represent you on the first day you have a product or service to sell.

# Chapter 22

# Recession: Your Greatest Opportunity

Some time ago, following a speaking engagement in Houston, I was having dinner with a group of entrepreneurs and their spouses. They talked a lot about the Recession, which was then in full bloom, and the effect it was having on them and their companies. I think everyone at the table, except me, was surprised to learn that every one of them was in the process of making major expansions in their companies. I wasn't surprised, because I had been traveling all over this land talking to entrepreneurs. Over and over I heard, "What recession?"

As a matter of fact, I had just returned from the Entrepreneur of the Year national affair in Boca Raton, Florida. During that three-day affair, with more than 1,000 people in attendance, there were a number of surveys taken, one of which dealt with expectations—89 percent of the entrepreneurs gathered there expected to expand their company the next year. When the results were announced, there was a stunned silence. The guy sitting next to me exclaimed, "Hell, since all I ever hear is recession, recession, I just assumed that my company was a part of a tiny minority that was still growing." So it went—so it goes, all over the country. Big companies and their media crying the blues, while entrepreneurs just keep their heads down and go on building their companies.

It all makes sense, if you think about it for a moment. What do big companies do in a recession? Well, of course, they retrench, cut back on advertising and on services, fire people, close divisions, withdraw products, and so on. What does all that add up to? They abandon "niches." And those niches, my friend, are the seedbeds for entrepreneurial growth. Recession is a time for all you entrepreneurs out there to listen attentively while your friends from large companies tell their sad and mournful stories. Maybe you should even shed a tear or two for them. Then get up, and go clobber them.

So, don't feel bad when you read in the business section of your local newspaper—or hear on national television—that the country is going to hell in a handbag. Just disregard the whole mess, because as sure as there's a cottonmouth moccasin in the Okefenokee Swamp, they ain't talking about you. How could they, when the media don't even know you and your kind are alive? Just remember, for the last decade, we have been the silent subset of the economy that has prevented this country from sinking into another depression like the infamous one of the '30s. But come to think about it, I guess most of you weren't even born way back then. In fact, maybe your mothers weren't either. But I was.

## Hobo jungle

So, let me tell you what it was like, back before the Entrepreneurial Revolution, when we depended on large companies to create jobs. We hear a lot today about the homeless. Well, we had them then, too. About 20 times as many per capita, as we do today. We just called them something different—"hobos." And I was one of them. For one long and miserable year of my life, in 1938, I lived in hobo jungles, rode in box cars with whole families—mothers, fathers and little babies wandering like nomads all over the country looking for enough food for just one more meal. I can't tell you how horrible it was. But I can tell you, that I learned the indignity of begging for food. Yes, and stealing it too.

That's where we would be today, were it not for you entrepreneurs along with your brothers and sisters around this country who've been responsible for practically all of the new jobs. George Bush told us, when he accepted the nomination, that in the immediate preceding eight years—the Reagan Years—that there had been 17 million jobs created. What he did not say was that during the exact same period, the Fortune 500 lost 3.5 million jobs. If it hadn't been for America's entrepreneurs and the 20 million net new jobs that *they* created, guess where we'd be today? Right back in the '30s.

Speaking of the Fortune 500, during the last five years over one-third of them have disappeared. Did you know that it took the previous 25 years for the same one-third to disappear? And guess who is replacing them? Well, of course, it is the same entrepreneurs who nobody knows are alive. Not the media. Not the banks, and certainly not our government. When will they wake up and start doing something to help the lonely and terrified individuals who are making the difference?

Just think what our economy would be like today if our legislators and the bureaucratic idiots who regulate banks were doing something to help entrepreneurs grow their companies, instead of passing laws to put us out of business. It's enough to make a Baptist preacher stop talking.

## Summary

With all the downsizing and cutbacks by large corporations, *now* is the time for entrepreneurial expansion.

## Lesson

Recession is the best time for entrepreneurs to expand. Get moving.

# Chapter 23

# Can You Be Bought?

There are a lot of *acquisition idiots*, who think they can *buy* entrepreneurs. There are a lot of entrepreneurs who believe they can sell *in* to large companies. When the two get together, disaster strikes. I couldn't care less about the *idiots*, but I have some well-earned advice to entrepreneurs who believe they can sell their company and keep on trucking. Oh what fools these mortals be!

Today's cash crunch, produced and directed by our stupid, insensitive government, is forcing thousands of entrepreneurs to do the unthinkable: sell their companies. If they sell *out*, that's one thing. If, for whatever the reasons, they grab the loot and head for the hills, so be it. But that's not what normally happens. When most large companies go out to buy an entrepreneur's business, they invariably have two conditions: First, get control. Second, keep entrepreneurial management *intact*. That's about as stupid as thinking that if you de-fang a rattlesnake, it can become a house pet. Without fangs, it ain't a rattlesnake. Without control, an entrepreneur ain't an entrepreneur anymore.

Yet, even as we speak, thousands of "de-fanged" entrepreneurs are joining bureaucratic snake farms. Everybody loses. The entrepreneur will either leave or become a drone. What was a fast-growing, entrepreneurial company is now a headless, nonproductive liability. How sad! What a waste!

I recently joined the board of a company intent on acquiring other companies. When advised of its strategy, I was astounded. The company targeting fast-growing, entrepreneurial companies in need of funds to grow on—invest $3 to $5 million; own at least 51 percent, but allow the entrepreneur to remain "in charge," with a long-term employment contract.

Whoa! In a private meeting with the chairman, I gave him a dissertation on acquiring entrepreneurs: You can buy entrepreneurs *out*, but you cannot buy them *in*. If you buy them out, be prepared to replace top management. There's a time to buy and a time *not* to buy. You buy only if a company is *mature*; only if the entrepreneur has truly delegated responsibility; only when professional management can take over. You do not buy when the company is still run day-to-day by the founding entrepreneur or when the company still needs entrepreneurial drive.

I explained that by limiting investments to $5 million, he had unwittingly targeted the very companies that probably should *not* be acquired, companies that would die without their entrepreneurs. I also protested long-term employment contracts for entrepreneurs. Slavery is illegal and you can't buy spirit.

The chairman asked, "What should we do?" I told him, "Raise your ante to $30 million; look for mature companies; buy entrepreneurs out; replace them unless they have become professional managers and are mentally conditioned to taking orders. That's a rare breed."

I wasn't lecturing the chairman from some book. Oh no! I've been there, in spades.

After I sold Formula 409, flush with money, I had a "great" idea. Since I had been a food broker most of my life, I designed a strategy to purchase local food brokers all over the country; to create the nation's largest organization selling to supermarkets; to put the ownership of all the companies in a single corporation—Harrell Sales, Inc.; to go public and make millions.

For those of you who don't know what a food broker is, let me explain: A food broker acts as the local sales and promotional arm for almost all companies who sell consumer products to supermarkets and mass merchandisers. Company representatives make presentations to buyers, then do all the detail work of building displays and fighting for shelf space. A food broker also develops cooperative advertising and promotional activity in local markets—and representatives work strictly on commissions, usually 3 to 5 percent. It's a great business.

## Don't be an idiot

For two years, I went around the country buying food brokers, each and every one run by a died-in-the-wool entrepreneur. Their organizations ranged in size from 10 employees to 300. I ended up buying 60 companies with combined sales in excess of $300 million. Great idea, right? Wrong. Double-damn wrong. Everything was great until it came time for the local companies, still run by their entrepreneurs, to "pass" money upstairs. Suddenly, everybody who had a Ford needed a Buick. Cadillacs replaced Buicks, Mercedes replaced Cadillacs. Hunting lodges, duck clubs, even yachts, became business necessities. The more they made, the more necessities they seemed to require.

You see, those entrepreneurs had been bought *out*. I thought I had bought them *in*. They were a lot more interested in their individual well-being and animal comforts than corporate goals or bull-philosophy about "building equity," or "times-earning ratios." I pleaded, I begged, I cajoled, I would have threatened, but they all had five-year employment contracts and I knew where I would be told to "stick it."

After three years of watching incredible growth in volume, in personnel and, above all, in "necessities," I raised my white and bloodied flag. I sold the companies back to the entrepreneurs I had bought them from, all unprofitable. One year later, such an amazing thing had happened: Every company was back making money, instead of losing it. You'll notice I didn't say profits, just more money for entrepreneurial necessities. It took a while, but I got paid, even made a profit, but never enough to pay for what I went through. I did learn a lesson. Only an idiot will try and buy an entrepreneur *in*.

So, my entrepreneurial friends, take heed. If the dog—or banker—is barking at the door, if the curtain is about to fall, if selling's all that's left: Get the cash. Repeat: Get the cash—*now*. Never a payout based on profits. Do not listen to all that bull about being part of a great team. Just smile when they tell you, "Nothing will change." They lie. And above all, don't kid yourself. Don't think you can take orders from nincompoops. *You* lie. Agree, if you must, to consult. Never sign an employment contract with slave owners. Remember what you are—an entrepreneur. You will be back.

## Summary

An entrepreneur cannot be bought. Any company that thinks it can buy an entrepreneur "in" with a long-term employment contract is headed for disaster.

## Lesson

If you're an entrepreneur and want to sell out, take the cash and run.

# All God's
# Dangers

# Chapter 24

# Protect Yourself From Bankruptcy Before It's Too Late

For those companies with great banking connections or incredible financial statements, the Recession may be ending. But for many entrepreneurs, the worst is yet to come. In fact, I predict there will be more bankruptcies filed by entrepreneurs in the next few years than in any other like period And, as amazing as it sounds, it will have little to do with how well those companies are run. Of course, you and I know it won't happen to *you*. But unless you are very rich or own your own bank, the danger may be very real. Why not take a moment and think "what if?" A small dose of preventive medicine can make the difference between personal disaster and entrepreneurial survival.

Let me explain: There are two economic forces coming together in America with a devastating "bang" on small and fast-growing companies.

First, banks are gobbling each other up like sharks in a feeding frenzy. The very banks that support entrepreneurs are disappearing, along with the loan officers who were there in the "beginning." Second, bank regulators and examiners have become little tin gods, and they are forcing every commercial bank in the country to reevaluate every loan. All of which means that your friendly loan officers are a disappearing breed, or they are growing bureaucratic horns and fangs. Don't be surprised if your new loan officers sit there filing their nails and looking out the window while you plead for time, or just one more renewal. Take my word, if it hasn't happened to you, it could. So why not prepare for the worst and pray I'm wrong?

Recently, I was with a friend of mine, John, an entrepreneur who was running a successful company in Dallas. Three years ago, he had developed a "niche" product that allowed him to successfully compete with a couple of national giants. He had put together a team of racehorses and was growing like the devil. Sales and margins were great. As a matter of fact, if he slowed his growth, he could have been showing a substantial profit. But like any self-respecting entrepreneur, John was reinvesting everything to satisfy his appetite for growth.

Everything was great—until he paid a visit to his bank for a quarterly review. Before he could explain his plans for continued growth, his loan officer advised him that as a result of a recent visit by the *little tin gods*, his loan had been "qualified." Not only could he not renew, he was asked to immediately reduce the loan. That wasn't possible since John had already hocked everything he owned—at least once. He protested, he pleaded, he pointed out that he had met every past commitment to the bank. His loan officer suggested that John seek other banking connections. Terror had just joined another meeting.

As John's story unfolded, I could see the final page—entitled, "Chapter 11." Because he was my friend, I told him so. After about an hour of considering options, John reluctantly admitted that I was probably right. "What, if anything," I asked, "have you done to prepare for this?" The answer? "Nothing. What the hell, Wilson, I didn't know until a few hours ago that it was going to happen."

## Get in the driver's seat

With those words, he joined millions of other entrepreneurs who may one day look back and say, "How could I have been so stupid?" I asked my friend if he knew what would happen to him, personally, on his first day in a bankruptcy court. Of course he didn't. I enlightened him: One of the first things the judge will ask you is, "What is your salary?" Regardless of what you say, the judge will tell you that as of the next day, your salary will be cut by one-half or more. When you try to explain that you honestly can't live on that, he'll join your banker and start filing his fingernails.

Disaster. *Stupid* disaster. Chapter 11 may have been inevitable, but if John had taken a dose of prevention, the scenario would be different. If he had but entered into a formal employment contract with his company, and then taken a double dose by having that contract collateralized by specific assets of the company, with proper UCC filings, he would be a "secured" creditor, with first rights of ownership to whatever assets had been pledged. If he had been wise enough to pledge something like the brand name of the company's product or the *patent* on the product, he would have been able to get out his own fingernail file and respectfully tell the judge and the credit committees and their lawyers and accountants (all being paid by the company), who was in charge.

If my friend had taken just a few hours to develop a well-conceived, and legally binding plan, it could have made the difference between survival and total disaster—to say nothing of what he'll have to go through explaining to his wife about giving up her company car, or why a smaller house (or room) will bring them and their four children closer together. John may still have time to get his medicine down before he is forced to file. I hope so. You can bet he's out there trying.

The reason I know all about this little flirtation with bankers and bankruptcy is that I have been there. Of course, if you have been an entrepreneur as long as I have, you have been almost everywhere. I like to think that every experience is another chapter in our entrepreneurial book of knowledge. But I must admit, I don't want any more chapters on "Going Bankrupt," and, believe me, you don't either.

So stop. Do not pass "Go." Find the best bankruptcy lawyer in town, spend a couple of hours thinking about and planning for what you know can never happen. Do it now.

## Summary

All entrepreneurs are facing tough times with their bankers. Perfectly good loans may be called. Disaster may strike. Why not expect the worst and protect yourself from the ills of bankruptcy?

## Lesson

Be sure you have a valid, enforceable employment contact, secured with critical company assets. It may make the difference between survival and personal disaster.

# Chapter 25

# Entrepreneurial Insurance

I get a lot of calls from entrepreneurs. Most are inspiring, but last week I listened to a horror story from Tom, an entrepreneur who had lost his company. He had started a company, done well for seven years, but then disaster struck. He tried everything to recoup, but now he was broke and forced to consider every entrepreneur's nightmare—working for somebody else. When I hung up, I realized, "There, but for the grace of God go I." And every other entrepreneur on this planet, including *you*, my friend.

One of the great sins we entrepreneurs commit is doing absolutely nothing to insure our future. Isn't it amazing? We pay enormous premiums for insurance to protect ourselves against everything conceivable. If our house burns down, we are insured. If there's a hurricane or flood, theft, fraud, illness, even death, we have insurance. But, like Tom, we have never given a moment's thought about our most devastating risk—financial collapse. I'll lay odds, you're in the same boat. So let's talk about what you could do.

Assume for a moment that an insurance company offered you a policy that would guarantee to finance you in a new venture if, God forbid, your present company went down the tube. What premiums would you be willing to pay for a policy that would protect your entrepreneurial integrity; against having to go on the job market; against having to work for somebody else? I don't know about you, but for me, the thought of not running my own company is simply not acceptable. No premium would be too much, if it protected my way of life. If you feel the same, let me share some thoughts.

There *is* insurance available. Not from any company, but from yourself. I call it "Entrepreneurial Insurance." A self-insured policy. The premiums can be adjusted to fit your particular circumstances. The effective date can be tomorrow. All that is required, old buddy, is for you to get off your haunches and do it.

But first of all, you've got to condition yourself. Go look in a mirror and have a heart-to-heart talk with that arrogant, conceited genius who's staring back at you. Tell him or her the following: "You are not invincible. You are not immortal. You can fail. Furthermore, you have a responsibility to your family. And above all, you most assuredly have a responsibility to yourself." Keep talking: "You are no different than all the other entrepreneurs in the world, most of whom will fail two or three times before they make it to the pearly gates. And when you fail, you will have to restart from scratch, begging money from every one you know." Keep talking until you accept the harsh reality that if your business fails, your entrepreneurial future could be gone with the wind.

## Blessed be the tithe

The next step is to get on your hands and knees, clasp your hands around a Bible, turn your face upward and take a solemn oath: "I swear that I will 'tithe' a part of my company's profits each month to insure my entrepreneurial future. I further swear that I will put those funds someplace where no one can ever get their hands on them. People like: lawyers, bankers, creditor, spouse—and especially *me*, unless this business fails."

127

Now don't tell me about your company not making any profits. Take it off the top, a small percentage of gross income. And don't tell me you can't afford it, not unless you've canceled all your other policies, including life, health and homeowner insurance. It's not important what percentage—of what—you take, just that paying the premiums becomes a sacred obligation. It should be the first bill you pay every month. And I'm talking about from *day one* of your entrepreneurial life. You decide how much, but take something out of the company every month and buy *entrepreneurial insurance.*

## Hide the loot

Where do you put it? Well, I don't want to try to practice law— although I've paid enough to buy a doctorate degree—but I can tell you there are a hundred ways to skin that cat. Nothing illegal, or even immoral, just loopholes in all those stupid laws that our inspired representatives have passed to take every flipping thing we own, if we ever dare make a mistake. So tomorrow, go find the most creative tax lawyer in your area of the country—preferably, one that specializes in estate planning—and start your own program.

I don't always practice what I preach, but entrepreneurial insurance is something I've always carried, to this day. My first plan was so simple: I borrowed money from a local bank and bought farm and forest land in Georgia... in the name of my children. I repaid the bank with monthly installments. When that loan was repaid, I borrowed again and bought more land. If my company had failed, I had a sure source of funds to start a new family business. Today, in addition to a family trust, I have a part-time job, running a small, income-producing company that is 100-percent owned by my young son.

Obviously, you can't buy entrepreneurial insurance without estate planning. But if you're like 90 percent of the entrepreneurs in America, that's something you've been putting off—waiting for your ship to come in, waiting until you have an estate. Well, that's just plain stupid. The day to start planning is the day you declare yourself to be an entrepreneur. Because on that day you started down an irreversible road. Take my word. You cannot go back. All bridges are burned. If you don't believe me, I'll give you Tom's number. You can call and talk to him.

## Summary

Entrepreneurs are born optimists. Yet things do go wrong. Assume the worst and insure yourself against disaster by putting a nest egg where even you can't get it.

## Lesson

The most important insurance policy in your portfolio is the one that will guarantee your ability to get up and fight again as an entrepreneur.

# Chapter 26

# Hold the Ego: Why You Need an Outside Board

As I travel around the country, speaking to and about entrepreneurs, I am often asked whether entrepreneurs should have outside members on their board of directors. My answer is a resounding *yes*, providing the company is past startup. Let me give you some thoughts.

First of all, let's examine ourselves for a moment. What special qualities do entrepreneurs have that allow them to do what everyone else knows can't be done? To climb hills that can't be climbed? The list is long, but it will surely include being a self-assured decision-maker— being aggressive, dedicated, creative, single-purposed, hard-working, confident and a positive thinker.

Now anyone who possesses all those qualities must have a little ego. Arrogance is probably a better word. Taking advice is not something that comes easily for most entrepreneurs, and for good reason. Because we know that if we had listened to all the "great" advice from our well-wishing friends, we'd never have started climbing the hill in the first place. We would never have joined the Club of Terror. Why on earth, then, should any self-respecting entrepreneur who has walked the lonely plank and successfully launched a business start listening to anybody? The answer? Because we are egomaniacal. But whether we like it or not, there comes a time when we need to listen. When? Good question. Let's talk about it.

In the beginning, during startup, I don't think an entrepreneur should listen to anybody except his or her innermost self. Now that doesn't mean that you don't research the hell out of whatever project you're working on, nor does it mean you don't discuss your idea with anyone who will listen. But in the final analysis, it's your gut feeling that should have the final vote. That will be your introduction to "loneliness." Get used to it. You'll live with it all the days of your life.

## Odd man "in"

But let's move ahead. Let's assume you've found a niche and it's working. Your company is growing. The chances are you'll run out of money. You'll need an investor—other than Mom and Dad. You'll start listening then, whether you like it or not. "First investors" also have some special qualities: In addition to wanting some *control*, they insist on giving advice, which is almost always wrong, because all they think about is short-term profit. If they have their way, you might as well start singing the entrepreneurial death chant.

There is a better way: *Appoint a board of directors.* Nothing complicated. Just you, the investor and an "outsider" that you both agree on. I didn't say it would be easy, but anything is better than having a "pain-in-the-rear" investor trying to call shots; or even worse, having the company go down the tube while the two of you argue.

Now let's move along to the next stage. The company keeps growing and you gradually staff up with vice presidents of everything. You have now reached *corporate maturity*. At this point you should start running your company as though it were *public*, even if you're still *private*, and intend to stay that way. Even if you were lucky enough to have never needed an investor and own all the stock, you should still run your company as if you had 1,000 investors.

131

It's time for a board of directors. I don't mean a bunch of vice presidents who know they'll either vote yes or resign. I'm also not talking about a "board of relatives." I'm talking about an honest-to-God board of directors, with *outsiders*. Now when I say outsiders, let me qualify that. No bankers or lawyers or accountants. No *anybody*, unless they have had to make payroll—without money, and know what it means to live without sleep. In other words, I believe that entrepreneurs should have mostly other entrepreneurs on their boards.

I didn't always feel positively about an outside board. As a matter of fact, I would probably never have had one, if it hadn't been forced on me by Wall Street when I bought Formula 409, Inc., which was a public company. Of course, I "loaded" it with employees and personal friends. I got out of that board, exactly what I deserved. Nothing.

Then I became a minority, but substantial, shareholder in another public company; I got myself elected to that board. After the first meeting, I was thoroughly disgusted. Everything was railroaded by the chairman. Resolutions were passed before I could vote yea or nay. I felt used and useless. Then it dawned on me, that's exactly how *my* board operated.

The next stockholders' meeting, we elected 11 members; myself and my president were the only insiders. Most of the other members were CEOs of entrepreneurial companies. From that day until today, I have never been chairman or member of any board that wasn't a "working" board.

## The entrepreneur's advantage

I am currently a director of four companies—two public, two private. Our meetings are very formal. We meet quarterly. The agenda is well-planned. The compensation and audit committee members are *outsiders*. Outside directors are paid a nominal fee and have stock options. What does the company get in return? Simple. It gets directors who work very hard for the company. The chairman has the incredible advantage of discussing ideas and problems with other entrepreneurs who have already been there. I can't count the times that the advice and counsel I have given—and received—has made an incalculable difference to the company.

When I think back on what my outside directors have meant to me, I am awed by how much the scales are balanced in my favor. Not only the mistakes I didn't make, but the incredible contacts and introductions and doors that were magically opened, particularly when I needed money. Bankers and investors love outside boards. Wall Street insists.

So if you're running a fast-growing company, stop for a moment. Ask yourself, what price ego?

## Summary

An outside board of directors composed of other entrepreneurs is an incredible source of knowledge and contacts for any fast-growing company. Every entrepreneur should have one.

## Lesson

If your company is past startup, go find one or more entrepreneurs who have been where you are going to serve on your board of directors.

# Chapter 27

# Entrepreneurs and Financial Advisors

If through some magic we could bring together all the entrepreneurs in the world—living and dead—and ask them, "In your life as an entrepreneur, what did you hate the most?" The answer would be an ear-piercing roar: *"Trying to raise money!"* Just the mention of words like "banker," "venture capitalist" and "Wall Street" would cause uncontrolled shivers of dread to run through the entire audience. Now ask yourself, "In my career, where have I been least effective?" If the answer is not, *"Trying to raise money,"* then you're not a normal entrepreneur.

Now let's change the scenario. Let's bring together all the bankers, venture capitalists and Wall Streeters—even the ones we wish were not among the living—and ask them, "In your career, who has made you the most money?" The begrudging answer would have to be, *"Entrepreneurs."* If you don't believe me, go get *The Wall Street Journal* and just try to find any company listed there that wasn't started by some lonely, terrified entrepreneur. Now let's ask them another question, "Among all your clients, who do you distrust the most?" The answer, of course: *"Entrepreneurs!"*

## Worlds apart

How is it possible for two groups of people—who are so dependent on each other—to distrust, even detest, the other so much? The problem is *mindset*. Let's take a moment to compare them: *They*, the money providers, believe with every morsel of their being that "growth" and "profits" are the same words; that "net revenue" is the only barometer for success. The idea that a business person would pour every dime of potential profit back into growing a company is simply not acceptable.

On the other hand, entrepreneurs know that showing a profit and paying taxes is stupid during the fast-growth years of a company. The word "risk" to the financial community is synonymous with Black Friday, AIDS, the Bubonic Plague and getting fired. To entrepreneurs, "risk" is a way of life—we eat it for breakfast. To entrepreneurs, "security" means the "company," and its continued growth. To *them,* it means mortgages on homes, liens on everything that's not nailed down and, above all, "personal guarantees." To *them* "success" means "pay back." To entrepreneurs, it means footprints in the sands of time. On and on it goes. Mindsets from different worlds.

## Oh no, not *you!*

To me, all of this adds up to an inescapable conclusion: Entrepreneurs should not attempt to interface with members of the financial community. If you know in advance that the chances of "getting along" are small to nil, why risk blowing a relationship that's so vitally important? Wouldn't it be better to employ the services of someone who could speak for you—someone with *their* mindset— someone who could act as interpreter? Just think of what it would mean if, throughout your entrepreneurial life, you had someone looking over your financial shoulder telling you "when," "who" and "how." I'm not talking about waiting around until the day you need money. I'm talking about finding such a person very early in your entrepreneurial career. If you wait until desperation is knocking, that's what will come through the door. I'm also not talking about hiring a financial vice president. That's a different issue.

I am a living example of what entrepreneurs should *not* do. I have run 10 major enterprises. In every case, there came a time when I desperately needed money to keep growing. Like most entrepreneurs, I always waited until the dog was barking at the gate before I started scurrying around, looking for money. Sometimes I was lucky. Other times I watched, in entrepreneurial horror, as perfectly good ideas went down the drain. Even when I solved my financial problems, I paid too much; gave up too much; or delayed my growth.

Now, in retrospect, I know that—way back in the beginning—I should have found my personal interpreter to the financial community. I should have made him or her an integral part of my entrepreneurial life, sharing my dream about conquering new worlds, as well as my horrible financial statement. When it came time to make presentations to bankers, venture capitalists or underwriters, my interpreter should have been the one to make the contacts and explained how I could, in fact, do what couldn't be done.

How could I have paid this individual? Simple. By letting him or her make commissions from every facet of my company's financial endeavors; making all our investments; recommending commercial banks and negotiating on our behalf; placing all our insurance needs; being the principal negotiator for acquisitions. I would have expanded that responsibility to include my personal estate planning and financial activity. Sure, he or she would have made a lot of money, but I would have saved a *thousand* times that much.

Of course the question is: Where to find that individual? Well, if I didn't already know someone, I'd go to the yellow pages and look under "Investment Bankers." I'd start with the largest and most reputable firm in my community. I'd try to meet with the local managing partner. My story would go something like this: "I'm an entrepreneur on my way to becoming a major factor in my industry. I want to select a financial advisor now, who'll become involved with me and help steer our company's financial course. I'm prepared to make meaningful, long-term commitments." What do you think the answer would be? Will they decline? I don't think so. If they do, go the next company on your list. Keep on talking until someone says yes.

During my time as publisher of *Inc.* magazine and, after that, as national chairman of The Council of Growing Companies, I've had an opportunity to deal with a lot of people in the financial community who are looking for entrepreneurs. Merrill Lynch is a sponsor of The Entrepreneur of the Year program—along with Ernst & Young. Smith-Barney-Shearson is a strategic partner of The Council of Growing Companies. Both are spending a lot of money and effort trying to reach the Entrepreneurial Market. I would be shocked if their local partners were not interested in the kind of proposition I have outlined.

During your entrepreneurial life, you are destined to pay a lot of money for financial services. You can be stupid and do as I did. Or you can be brilliant and do as I *say*.

## Summary

Entrepreneurs and members of the financial community simply do not speak the same language. Doesn't it make sense to find an interpreter to speak on your behalf?

## Lesson

Every entrepreneur will someday be forced to raise money. Be smart and employ the services of a member of the financial clan to represent you.

# Chapter 28

# Solving Legal Problems

I am convinced that my greatest waste of time and money as an entrepreneur involved solving legal problems. If I had the money I've paid lawyers to bring legal actions against perpetrators and defend myself against lawsuits, I'd be a *jillionaire*. What irks me the most is that in practically every case, the suits were settled—but only after I'd paid enormous fees and costs. My lawyers were the only winners.

I'll resist the temptation to stop here and tell you my 100 lawyer jokes; but if you know any new ones, fax them to me. In fairness, lawyers are retained to take our side. They don't last very long unless they tell us we're right, and assure us we'll win. Off to war we go, armed with all the emotions that warriors take to the battlefield: kill, kill, kill. The determination to win overshadows logic, and so begins the exodus of funds from our bank account, and a sinful diversion of entrepreneurial talent, time and energy away from company business. Oh how clever we are!

There must be a better way... and there is. I was talking recently with Jack Linkletter, the son of my best friend Art Linkletter. Jack, like his father, is a world-class entrepreneur. He has founded a very successful company in Irvine, California: Productive Conflict Management (PCM). As the name implies, he is in the business of resolving conflicts, before lawyers and emotions take over. What a great idea!

I don't know how many such companies now exist, but it's bound to be an explosive new service industry. What could be more simple or expedient than having both sides submit their position in a conflict to a disinterested, wise and experienced counselor? Just think. No more depositions, interrogatories, court reporters, judges—or lawyers. Just people solving business problems. Just think of the money and time saved by settling in a day or two, as opposed to years of legal battles... to say nothing of all the emotional wear and tear.

## Kangaroo's court

I'm reminded of a lawsuit I wish I could forget—my first courtroom experience, many years ago. I acquired a company that continued to operate as a wholly owned subsidiary of our company. The founder of the company remained as president and chief operating officer, with a five-year employment contract. That was before I learned that you can't buy an entrepreneur *in*. Shortly, we discovered that our president was a regular and confirmed partaker of "the fruit of the vine." He drank at home, at the office, with or without customers. This condition was aggravated by the impact of alcohol on his propensity for sexual activity—at the office, with or without customers.

After repeated warnings, we fired the guy. He sued. About two years later, after exorbitant legal expenses, we went to trial. The first thing I learned was that the inalienable right guaranteed to us by our forefathers, "to be tried by your peers," is a joke. The jurors ranged from the unemployed to the unemployable. All the corporate executives, company owners and everybody else who was gainfully employed had been excused. We didn't have the chance of the proverbial snowball. We lost. Not because we didn't have the legal right to fire, but because we were big and rich compared to every single member of the jury. When I think back over that experience I realize that I could have settled the whole thing for one-tenth of what it finally cost me if I had used a Jack Linkletter.

## Confine conflict

I wish Jack well. His company is doing something that's truly needed in America. Today, we hear a lot about containing health costs and I agree something should be done. But for entrepreneurs who are trying to grow their companies, I believe the containment of legal expenses is just as important. So, when the next conflict raises its ugly head, and just before you hire a lawyer to tell you how *right* you are, go find your Jack—some company like PCM—and get the problem quickly and economically resolved. If you can't find a company, then get with your adversary and create your own. Find a retired judge or, better yet, a retired CEO, and ask him or her to adjudicate the conflict. They probably won't be as inventive or creative as a professional firm like Jack's, but anything is better then pouring money down a rat hole.

So, all you entrepreneurs out there, hear me now—the wiser, poorer voice of experience: *Stay the hell out of courtrooms!*

## Summary

Entrepreneurs waste too much time and money fighting lawsuits that end up being settled, and even more when they go to trial. There are now professional companies that are experts in solving conflicts *before* they become lawsuits.

## Lesson

When conflict raises its ugly head—and it will—get the problem solved by some outside arbitrator before a lawsuit is filed.

# Chapter 29

# The Enemy Within

The other day I received a telephone call from a lawyer, which is enough to ruin anyone's day. In this case, it was a voice out of the past, a man who used to work for me. The call was unimportant, just asking for a contribution. However, it stirred up some memories of a "happening" that most entrepreneurs will face sooner or later.

During my career, I have faced disaster more times than I care to remember. Some were self-inflicted. Others were initiated by outside forces over which I had no control. But the episodes I'll never forget are the times my senior executives, the people I trusted most, made "moves" against me or the company. If that hasn't happened to you, it will. So listen while I tell you a tale of woe. See if you recognize any of the players.

The story begins at a small Southern town in the early '60s, when I met and engaged a young lawyer to handle some real estate transactions for me. I was tremendously impressed with his ability. Our relationship ripened from lawyer-client to friendship. It was obvious to me that he, as a small-town lawyer, was wasting his talents.

For me, it was an exciting time. My worldwide military sales company was thriving, with offices throughout America and in 15 foreign countries. In addition, I had acquired Formula 409 out of bankruptcy and we were well on the way to becoming a national brand. Our in-house attorney had recently resigned. We were looking for a replacement. I had our man. Let's call him Zack. He left his small town, moved to New York and became my most trusted vice president, and more. We were like brothers.

By 1971, a lot of great things had happened. Formula 409 had become the nation's number-one spray cleaner. We had merged our military sales company with Formula 409 to form Harrell International, Inc., completed a very successful public offering, sold 409 to Clorox, and moved the company to Jacksonville, Florida. Zack had done well, in every respect. His financial house had grown, along with his ability. From small-town lawyer, to a highly respected executive VP and corporate attorney. As one of three inside directors of a 13-member board, he was responsible for all stockholder relations and interfacing with our outside directors.

## Down the drain

The years 1972 and '73 were not good for Harrell International. When 409 was sold, we suddenly had $7 million in cash—back in the days when $7 million was a lot of money. Unfortunately, we received some bad tax advice. We were told that unless the proceeds from the sale was re-deployed within 120 days, we were in danger of having the IRS impose an excess profit tax on the unnecessary accumulation of reserve. The only answer was to buy companies; anything, just get the money reinvested.

There was a wrinkle: We had to buy "operating" companies; passive investments would not qualify. Now, an entrepreneur with an open checkbook is a disaster looking for a place to happen under any circumstances. But trying to get rid of $7 million in 120 days was a challenge. I went around buying anything that moved: ranches, marinas, construction companies, even an insurance agency. When the acquisition spree was over, we no longer had to worry about the IRS.

However, we developed another small problem: We began losing money. That was followed by our stock tumbling; followed by nasty letters from stockholders, hourly calls from Wall Street, requests for bank reviews; followed by a thoroughly angry board of directors, all of whom conveniently forgot that they had approved all my acts. Suddenly, entrepreneur Harrell was not having a good time.

Then one happy day, I was in the Texas hinterlands, trying to sell our ranch, when I returned a call to one of the few directors who would still speak to me. "Wilson," he asked, "What's this special directors' meeting all about?" "What meeting?" I asked. Silence, more silence. "What meeting are you talking about?" I asked again. Still no answer. Then, "Well, the only thing I know is that I received a registered letter, calling a special directors' meeting in New York for tomorrow morning at 9 a.m." I headed for New York.

I was 15 minutes late, the inevitable traffic jam. The directors were assembled. The agenda was not complicated or lengthy: *Replace president and CEO Harrell with new president and CEO—Zack.* With my unexpected arrival, the meeting was adjourned, followed by another directors' meeting with another simple agenda: *Fire Zack.*

Now I know you're thinking, "But nothing like that could ever happen to me." Bull! You say you don't have any "Zacks" working for you. More bull. This world is full of "Zacks." They come in every size and description, and they don't even have to be lawyers. If you'd like to meet a few, call all your executives together. The chances are that every one of them would like to have your job. If they don't, you'd probably do well to replace them with others who do. Wanting your job, plus being aggressive, is how you spell "success." It also spells "Zack." The question is not *if,* but *when* and *who.*

## Who's your Zack?

For all of you who are now giving me the old entrepreneurial finger, because you own 51 percent of the stock and can't be fired, stop smirking. "Zack" will do the same to you, just in a different way. You'll know when you get your call in Texas, and learn that a trusted employee has set up a competitive company, taking with him or her half of your customers and a few of the other "Zacks" you trusted so much. Hell, that's the way most entrepreneurs get started in the first place.

The moral of my story is *not* how to keep "Zacks" out of your organization—you can't build without them. And I'm not suggesting you try to change human nature. What I'm saying is know it will happen and be prepared. My mistake with Zack was simple. Because he was my close personal friend, I trusted him too much. I delegated to him something that no entrepreneurs should ever delegate—interfacing with directors and stockholders. That's almost as stupid as allowing any executive to become closer to your largest customer and/or supplier, than you are. Whatever your business, there are some tasks that must not be delegated.

My final bit of advice, *Keep alert.* Don't do what I did and get so caught up in your own ego that you overlook the "Zacks." My father was a world-class entrepreneur back when nobody, including him, could spell the word. He passed on some words of wisdom that I'd like to share: "Every morning of your life, before you leave home, go someplace and be alone. Ask yourself a question, 'Is there any SOB anywhere out there that can hurt me—today?' " If the answer is yes, that's the job you go take care of—first.

## Summary

Entrepreneurs are continually faced with having a trusted executive trying to take over part or all of their company. You can't build a company without surrounding yourself with bright and ambitious people. The very kind of people who want what *you* have.

## Lesson

Beware of those friends who have their arms around your neck. They may be in the act of strangling you.

# Chapter 30

# Unions and Entrepreneurs

There is probably nothing more horrifying for an entrepreneur than to suddenly find a union sniffing around his or her company. The very idea that one or more of your trusted employees might be plotting with the union to organize your company is devastating. If you're like most entrepreneurs, your first thought is to find out who the disloyal SOBs are and fire them. Of course, if you do that, you'll find out very quickly what it's like to have a pack of 800-pound gorillas attack you. They are, of course, part of our beloved government—another of those great agencies created and deployed to make life miserable for entrepreneurs.

## How to destroy a company

Once the unionizing process begins, the entrepreneur is in for some mighty black days and more sleepless nights. As I think back over my career, I can remember nothing that caused me such anger and frustration. It was back in the '80s. Our company had grown like the devil, and was responsible for sales in excess of $500 million.

We had a number of subsidiaries, one of which was located in San Francisco. It was a food brokerage company with about 75 employees, all of whom were salespeople and administrative staff. Now on the face of it, that surely is not a normal candidate for unionization. But as luck would have it, we had employed a secretary who was married to an organizer for the local Teamsters Union.

Out of the blue, our subsidiary was being organized. Our local executives were in a state of shock. They knew zip about labor law, so we retained a labor lawyer who suddenly started running the company. Just as suddenly, business came to a screeching halt. Nobody had time for such mundane things as selling and administering. They were too busy attending union meetings and politicking. Incredibly, the union won by a narrow margin.

I could, but won't, entertain you for the next hour or so, by fully describing the vocal and body language of an entrepreneur who has just been unionized. My descriptions of the players involved became increasingly creative as I watched, in horror, a great organization degenerate into a disgusting mess. The anti-union people stopped speaking to the pro-union employees. People stopped speaking to anyone, especially customers. Management couldn't give bonuses, or promote, or even give raises without checking with the union representative, who, not surprisingly, was the same secretary who had started the whole thing. I could go on and on. But suffice it to say, we sold that company. And predictably, it soon went out of business.

## Hindsight is 20/20

Back then, I blamed a lot of people. On reflection, the real culprit was *me*. We had become a large company employing a lot of people. And we were doing just what most big companies do. Making people into numbers. If I had known then what I know today, there is no way any union could have organized that company. If I had instilled an "entrepreneurial spirit" throughout our company; if I had encouraged creativity and allowed individuals to contribute; if I had recognized and rewarded entrepreneurial achievement; if I had allowed a sense of ownership to prevail and set our people free, then the need for protection would never have raised its ugly head. And there would never have been a union. But alas, I was just another big company CEO who got what he deserved.

## Unions had their day—yesterday

I know this all sounds as if I'm a born-again union buster. And I suppose I am. Having said that, let me also say that there was a time when unions were absolutely necessary. And lest we forget, all of us will forever be indebted to unions for what they have done for our country. Without unions, there would be no middle class in America— or the world. There would be no one to buy the product and services that we entrepreneurs are selling.

Without doubt, unions were the engines that cranked up the Industrial Revolution. But that revolution has been replaced by the Entrepreneurial Revolution, which—sooner or later—will be the death toll for unions. As a matter of fact, I doubt that there would be unions today if entrepreneurs remained entrepreneurs throughout their business careers. But unfortunately, as entrepreneurs arrive at phase three of their transition—the Disassociated Director, the "letting-go" phase—they stop being entrepreneurs and become simply CEOs of large companies, with bureaucrats putting a damper on every semblance of "freedom." A joyous day for unions.

When you get right down to it, the only thing a union does for its members is give them a chance to be heard. It may all start out being about wages and benefits, but that quickly grows into an insidious "joint tenure" between unions and corporate executives. So begins the beginning of the end.

But that was yesterday and today. Entrepreneurs of tomorrow will do it better. We are learning that *freedom*—from top to bottom— is the only passport to true visionary leadership.

## Summary

Entrepreneurs and unions simply don't go together. In fact, if entrepreneurs will remember who and what they are, then unions will cease to exist.

## Lesson

The best way to keep unions out of your company is to keep *freedom* in.

# Chapter 31

# Keeping the Spirit Alive

As entrepreneurs grow their companies, they get so embroiled in raising money, building an organization and selling, that they often fail to nurture and embrace the single most important quality that got them growing in the first place—the *Entrepreneurial Spirit*. The faster they grow, the more successful they become, the more that special ingredient is ignored. It's a nightmare to watch an entrepreneur self-destruct. Yet it happens, over and over again. So, listen up while I pass on some words of wisdom for which I paid dearly—and so will you, if you're not very careful.

There are two things that don't go together—big companies and entrepreneurship. Now, "big" is a relative term. For entrepreneurs it may be a company with just two people, so I'm not talking about General Motors. I'm talking about *you*, whatever your size. There is a disease—I call it "*anti*-preneur"—that inflicts every growing company.

It starts early and spreads like wildfire. By the time you're a Fortune 500 company, the disease can be terminal.

As a consultant, I am often retained by a large company to try to cure the "anti-preneur" plague. My assignment is two-fold: First to try and interpret for them the mindset of entrepreneurs, so they can be better prepared to deal with them in their marketing efforts; second, to help them instill in their organizations an entrepreneurial spirit.

The fact that I'm there is amazing. It wasn't long ago that the word "entrepreneur" was not used in corporate society. If you so much as uttered the word, and someone overheard, you didn't have to worry about your future. When I used to go to cocktail parties where corporate executives assembled, someone would inevitably ask me who I worked for. I would answer, "Nobody, I'm an entrepreneur." With that, everyone would move away from me. Suddenly I was drinking alone, like I had leprosy. Now, it's all different. Everybody wants some. I'm glad to sprinkle a little entrepreneurial light into some mighty dark places.

## A force to reckon with

On these assignments, at my very first meeting, I ask one of my favorite questions, "What do you think motivates an entrepreneur?" Since I already know the answers, I write them on a blackboard. Money. Power. Influence. I then erase the whole list and replace it with a single word: *Freedom*. I go on, "It is the quest for *freedom* that fuels the entrepreneurial spirit. Free to be your own person; free to get your head above the crowd; free to have an idea, and turn that idea into a company, and that company into an empire, if you can."

Freedom is such a simple word, yet the most powerful force in the history of mankind. I don't believe there's much difference between people who risked their lives jumping over the Berlin Wall and American entrepreneurs. Both were inspired by the same force—freedom.

But, what went wrong? Where did Corporate America lose its way? Our forefathers escaped the chains and shackles of foreign prisons to seek freedom in America, only to find themselves and their children's children, recaptured and rechained with more insidious implements of torture. We call them "golden handcuffs." They may be invisible, but the purpose is exactly the same.

How could large companies be so stupid? Don't they know from whence we came? That freedom is our birthright? Our genetic inheritance? Who on the earth ever dreamed up the idea that you can build a "team" by handcuffing employees? Of course, "golden handcuffs" are not the disease, they are but a symptom. The *disease* is the big-company philosophy that only executives are people, everybody else is a member of the great unwashed; that all wisdom resides at headquarters; that responsibility can be freely delegated—but never authority. Is it any wonder that Corporate America is in trouble? Every time you pick up a paper, the headlines tell of another large company trekking its way to its dinosaur's grave.

The foolish policies of large companies only worked so long as they were competing against each other, before the Entrepreneurial Revolution came along and changed the world. Today, these lumbering Goliaths have a new economic force to reckon with—a whole mess of Davids with rocks. Entrepreneurs who understand, first-hand, what *freedom* is all about. I have one bit of friendly and free advice for the CEOs of large companies: *Duck!*

# Reward risk

But forget big companies and their problems. Let's get back to *you*. Are you sure that you're not headed down the same path? As your company grows and you begin to delegate, be absolutely sure you delegate the Entrepreneurial Spirit to everyone. Make it common property. Don't ever let some professional human resources person persuade you to install some high-falutin' plan taught at Harvard or at some large corporation.

There is one, and only one, policy that will work. Just turn *freedom* loose. Remember, everyone working for you has an insatiable desire for freedom. All are endowed with an Entrepreneurial Spirit. Be sure that nobody puts a damper on that flame. Let everyone feel that they are making a contribution. That means letting them make decisions. Reward them for risk. Let them remain with the company because they want to, not because some genius dreamed up a clever way to imprison them. In the final analysis, money, power, influence, vacations and retirement are all fringe benefits. Freedom is a force. Employ it wisely and go kill giants. Then become one.

## Summary

The force that motivates entrepreneurism is *freedom*. Freedom to rise above the crowd to be your own man or woman. Freedom to have ideas and make those ideas into empires—if you can. Everything else is just a byproduct.

## Lesson

If you want to be an entrepreneur, be sure that your aim is to be free to do something well. To leave a footprint in the sands of time. And be sure you give your employees the freedom to make contributions, to earn rewards—and even make mistakes.

# Chapter 32

# What God Do You Worship?

Fortune 500 companies are biting the dust faster than tumbleweeds in a tornado. And guess what's replacing them? Entrepreneurs. Never before in recorded history has there been such economic turmoil—not in America, not in the world.

How is it possible for humongous companies, with all their resources, to get clobbered by a bunch of upstarts? For the last two decades, entrepreneurs all over the country, in every field of business endeavor, have been creating havoc in the economic world by replaying the David and Goliath story and "smiting" giants. The question is why. In search of an answer, let me share some thoughts with you.

I have been privileged to meet and become close personal friends with a lot of Fortune 500 CEOs. We have worked together and played together. We've shared frustrations, and celebrated successes. In the process, I got to know a lot about the mindset of the individuals who run Corporate America.

On the other side of the economic coin, I know an awful lot about America's entrepreneurs. Not only from my own personal experience of being a charter member of that clan, but for the past five years, I have spent most of my waking hours talking to, writing about, speaking for and consulting with more entrepreneurs than I can count.

It was in comparing Fortune 500 CEOs with entrepreneurs that led me to the conclusion that most of the giant companies in our country, and indeed the world, are dinosaurs just waiting for their food to run out. Of course, they will be replaced by other large species whose fate will be the same. On and on it goes, the same stupid history repeating itself. Successful entrepreneurs go about building small companies into giants, and then, unaccountably, follow their predecessors down the death march, into the world beyond. Again, the question: Why? Well, I think it's all about what business "god" is worshipped by whom—and when. Let me explain.

## Amen

When entrepreneurs take that first lonely and terrorizing step into the unknown, they inevitably do so because they discovered a product or service niche that was being taken for granted or ignored by the giants. Typically, they borrow money from anyone and everyone they know, and then somehow accomplish the impossible. They put together a team of racehorses and then, in spite of banks who hate them, and government who doesn't know they exist and competitors a hundred times bigger, they find customers and build a company.

Along the way, they do a lot of sweating and a lot of praying, but the only business "god" that entrepreneurs ever worship is the company's product and its customers and the people racehorses who share their dream. When the entrepreneurs get up in the morning, what do they think about? Their product: how to do it better or cheaper, or sell it to somebody new. About their "team" of dedicated people and the needs of their customers...Amen.

Now let's visit the CEOs who run Fortune 500 companies. What's their first thought in the morning? What business "god" do they worship? Do you think it's their company's product? No! Their customers? No way! Their people? Are you kidding? You and I know that their first act is to grab *The Wall Street Journal,* turn immediately to the stock listings and check to see what kind of report card their "god"— Wall Street—has given them. Heaven protect them if this quarter's earnings are less than a year ago. "God" will strike them dead. Dare they cut back on profits when the product is in trouble and needs help? Never! Not if it means breaking the only commandment in the Wall Street Bible—"Thou shall never make less profit than the previous period." Of course that bible doesn't have a Book of Revelation. If it did, it would have only one word: "Disaster."

But what does all this mean to you and me? Does it mean that entrepreneurs should never allow their companies to become large? Should they never, never "go public"? Is Wall Street the Great Satan? Is there no hope for a large company? The answer, of course, is no. A *resounding* no. What it does mean, pure and simple, is that regardless of size, an entrepreneurial CEO must never worship false gods. Never forget that the *product,* the *people* and the *customer* are what his or her company is all about. Is it easy? Let me assure you, from personal experience, it is not. I was CEO of a public company for some 25 years, and although the company was never a super giant, I got to know a lot about the Wall Street Bible—*including* the Book of Revelation.

When I bought Formula 409, it was a small public company that had gone "belly up"—because its owners had committed the unpardonable sin of spending all their money on advertising before they had distribution. We settled with the creditors for five cents on the dollar, and went about taking the product nationwide. I knew absolutely nothing about running a public company. I just kept my entrepreneurial head down, worked my butt off, put together a great team and built a company.

As sales and profits increased, I was introduced to Wall Street; specifically, the stockbrokers who were "making a market" for Formula 409 stock. I began to get visits and phone calls from bright young MBA'ers, asking all kinds of questions about the com-pany. But there was one question that was always asked by each of them, over and over, day after day: "What will your earnings be this quarter and how does that compare to the same quarter last year?" I talked about our great ideas, about our people, about how satisfied our customers were, about new worlds we would conquer. They smiled, nodded their collective heads and asked, "How about earnings this quarter?" As luck would have it, my answers were just what they wanted to hear and, boy-oh-boy, did they react! I watched in utter amazement as our stock soared. From 50 cents, to $2, then $4, then $8. Wall Street loved me.

## Up, up and away

There came a time when we needed money to keep growing. No problem. Wall Street was all over me. We did an offering at $14. Oversubscribed. More sales, more profits, every quarter up, up, up. Our stock? Up—$16, then $18, then $22. Our 409 stock was selling for an incredible 40-times earnings. Not only did Wall Street love me, *I* loved me, too. And why not? I was making paper money so fast I could hardly count it—but I tried. Every morning, my first act was to check *The Wall Street Journal* and see how much I had made since yesterday. What a joy! How wonderful to be so rich and so beloved by so many beautiful people. Executive dining rooms, gourmet food, vintage wines. Drinks at "21," dinner at the "in" places, with the "in" people, headwaiters bowing and scraping.

What a life, what an incredible life. There I was, not long out of the swamps of Georgia, now at the top of the world and eating mighty high on a big, fat hog.

But wait. What's was happening back at the company? What was going on with Formula 409? Well, that was no longer my concern. I'd done what all good CEOs do: I'd delegated. I hired a president, whose job was to worry about all the little details of running the company, and he had a lot of VPs running around taking care of things. *Me*, I had more important things to do. Without being aware of it, there had been a subtle, yet profound change in the mindset of entrepreneur Wilson Harrell. He had been converted and there was a new "god" to worship: Wall Street. I wasn't alone.

All this was in the '60s, at the beginning of the Entrepreneurial Revolution. Although there weren't many of us, we were sure chopping a lot of cotton. Some of those early entrepreneurs stayed and became great. Others faded into oblivion. I did something different: I woke up! One day, I had a conversation with my best friend and partner, Art Linkletter, who has introduced more new products than all the other show people on earth—put together. Art sat me down and explained what I was doing to myself, and to all those people who had shared my dream. The next time I shaved, I saw what *he* saw. A few months later, I sold the name 409 and the formula to Clorox. However, I did not sell the company. Not one of my people went with the deal. I also got back to being an entrepreneur. Hallelujah!

## Keep your faith

Hopefully, I've made my point. It's awfully easy to let the bright lights fool you, to get priorities confused. And when you do, don't look for someone to blame. In my case, I found the enemy—and it was *I*. The people I met on Wall Street were, for the most part, very competent and very sincere. Without them, 409 would never have become a household word. They were simply doing their job. Just ask yourself: When you get ready to buy publicly traded stock or a mutual fund, what questions do you ask? "How's their earnings?" "How does this quarter compare with the same quarter last year?" America has been taught to worship the one and only financial "god" in our universe: short-term profits. Is it right? Absolutely not! Is it good for our country? Not in a million years.

Let me pose an interesting question: Just what business "god" do you think the Japanese have been worshipping for the past couple of decades? Their *products*. What's wrong with General Motors, Ford, Chrysler and all the other giants that have been losing market share to superior Japanese products? Are the Japanese smarter? Do they have more money? Better ideas? More dedicated people? Of course not. They just know what business "god" to kneel to. For years and years they have been stealing our innovations, manufacturing them better and then shipping them back to us. Our best hope is that they will start opening more and more stock exchanges.

Having said all these bad things about large companies and Wall Street, let me also say that if I had it to do over, I would go public in a heartbeat. I think, in most cases, it's the best and safest way for entrepreneurs to raise capital for sustaining growth, providing they remember from whence they came as well as the simple Golden Entrepreneurial Rule: There is but one "god" in any business, and that "god" is the product. Hallelujah.

P.S. There's another false "god" roaming around out there, in the entrepreneurial world, that you need to be very careful of because he can zap your organization without you realizing he even exists. He's difficult to see, but if you look carefully, you may catch a glimpse of him the next time you pass a mirror.

## Summary

Entrepreneurs build their companies because they worship their *product* and *people* and *customers*. Meanwhile, large public companies are forced to worship profits and Wall Street. Unfortunately, as entrepreneurs grow and become giants, they copy the dinosaurs on their way to oblivion.

## Lesson

Entrepreneurs should always remember that their *product*, and *people* and *customers* are the only true business "god" to worship.

# Raising
# Entrepreneurs

# Chapter 33

# Entrepreneurs vs. Family

I want to start off by making two statements: First, the most wonderful partner any entrepreneur can have is a spouse. Second, the worst possible scenario for an entrepreneur is to have "family" involved in his or her company.

Although those statements seem like opposites, I believe both are true. How can that be? Good question. Let's talk about it.

I know that whatever I say will be wrong for a lot of people. There are exceptions. Incredible exceptions. But they just prove the rule.

If you are an entrepreneur in the startup mode, and you don't have your wife or husband aboard that shaky ship, you are nuts. Since you are going to live a life of broken dates, canceled vacations, missed games and school plays, you sure better have a partner at home. When I say *partner*, I am not talking about someone who is passively interested. Just the opposite. I am talking about a spouse who knows everything you know. Someone who loves you when the whole world thinks you're nuts. As I have said over and over, "entrepreneur" is just another word for unbelievable loneliness and stark-raving terror. Eventually, you'll learn how to live with those lifetime partners, but not in the beginning. A case in point:

When I got out of the Air Force in 1953, and started my company in England, I had $140, and a "great idea." I also had a wife, a baby and another on the way. Our flat had a stove, a bed and a baby crib. The rest of our furniture, including my office, was made up of orange crates with planks across them. We damn near starved to death, and would have had it not been for my wife selling her jewelry. Was my wife my partner? You bet she was. If the truth be known, I expect her terror was on an even higher plane than my own.

Six years and three children later, when I moved my wife into a 10,000-square-foot chateau in Paris, with seven servants, she had migrated from being a *partner* to knowing absolutely nothing about my business. And that's the point: In most cases, there's a time when spouses should leave the company. I can't tell you the date or year. I most assuredly can't tell you *how*. But I can tell you when and why.

The time for spouses to fade into their own world, is when the company begins to mature. When you are past startup. The day you hire your first vice president should be the beginning of the "fading" process. Hear me now, loud and clear: There can only be one boss in any company, and it must be *you*. If your wife or husband is in the company, you are "joint bosses," and there's nothing you can do or say that will convince your employees that the other one ain't calling the shots. And that goes for your bankers, suppliers, customers and, of course, your lawyers, who always know where the "power" lies.

I didn't say it would be easy, just necessary. In my case, I gradually persuaded my wife to be less involved with the company and more involved in family and community affairs. If that won't work for you, then go buy your spouse another business. Do what you have to do, but get your spouse out of the company. If things get desperate enough, let 'em run for office—that'll surely do the trick.

## Succession dilemma

Now a more serious discussion—children. As entrepreneurs, we want our children to follow in our footsteps. And why not? We live an incredible life, and we want the same for our offspring. But the very qualities that make us entrepreneurs make it difficult for us to bring our children along in the company. Even if we could, others in the company may object. Our children end up frustrated and angry at us.

Is there a way? Perhaps. In Europe the "fathers" long ago sent their sons off to serve apprenticeships with other craftsmen, until they were fully qualified to lead. Let your children go earn their stripes someplace *else* before you make them vice presidents, officers or directors. Incidentally, be sure they work for another entrepreneur. For God's sake, don't let some big company poison their minds and teach them all about the corporate ladder.

Finally, there's the problem with the rest of the family: in-laws, nieces, nephews, uncles, aunts. I know many who have worked miracles for entrepreneurs. But if you took a vote of all the executives working in companies with relatives, you would get words like: incompetent, stupid, lazy, etc. It's not important whether they're right, just that they think it and that "smells" up the whole place.

Incidentally, I have systematically broken every rule that I have just pontificated. I survived. So will you, because I think all this will go right through one ear and out the other. It would have for me, if I had been reading, instead of writing. Oh, to be an author!

## Summary

In the beginning, entrepreneurs need their families, particularly spouses, to be totally involved with the company. But as the company matures and executives are employed, it's time for the family to phase out.

## Lesson

When you hire your first vice president, it's time to start getting your family out of the company.

# Chapter 34

# Make Your Kid a *Real* Entrepreneur

Entrepreneurs come in every size, shape and description. Every conceivable background. From wealthy parents to upbringings of abject poverty. From rural farms to city slums. There is simply no consistency. Or is there? I think there is.

I believe that behind every entrepreneur is someone who "made it happen." Somebody who lit a flame that could never be put out. Who? Well, whoever loved them enough—normally, their parents. I believe that every mother and father holds in his or her hands the ability to inspire an entrepreneurial spirit in a child. So, if you have a child, face up to the fact that you control his or her ultimate destiny. You can't delegate that responsibility. Not to teachers or employers or any-one else. The making of an entrepreneur starts at home, and nowhere else. From the day a child is born, the outside world will be desperately trying to quash every semblance of the entrepreneurial spirit.

If you don't believe me, examine the curriculum at a local school. Try to find a course that teaches a student how to start a business. How to break the rules. How to march to a different tune. In what class are students taught the exhilaration that comes with creating a new product or building a company? Ask yourself, is there any place in the whole system that encourages your child to become an entrepreneur?

Now let's move ahead to the time our children get their first jobs. Do you know of any employer who attempts to teach employees how to become entrepreneurs? Perhaps in the future, but not yet.

# Nurturing the instinct

Add it all up, mothers and fathers. If you don't do it, it won't get done. Entrepreneurship is "home work," pure and simple. Now let's deal with the question of *how*. How can we breathe the entrepreneurial spirit into our children? By letting our sons and daughters be in business for themselves. That's another way of saying let them make decisions. From day one, throughout their lives, applaud every individual initiative and accomplishment, no matter how small. Turn chores into an exciting business venture. The great thing about this "at-home entrepreneurship" is that it's perfectly natural. From birth to death, all of us want to be creative and to contribute. Our problem is how to stop the world from stomping out that God-given instinct, particularly in young people, and turning us into "stompers."

# Boy oh boy

I'm an entrepreneur because my father made me one. He was a typical, small-town businessman. He owned farms, cotton gins, saw mills and a general store. I followed him around like a puppy on a leash. When I was 6 years old, I founded my first enterprise. A lemonade stand. My father gave me the money to buy lemons and sugar. I furnished the labor. Every month we split profits at a formal "sit-down" business meeting. When I gave my father his share, I was 9 feet tall. I ended up with six lemonade stands and a bank account in my name. When I was 7, I bought my father out. What a day that was!

Then, when I was 11, my father made me a cotton buyer at his gin. Let me explain: In those days, in our small rural community, the farmers grew cotton and tobacco as their cash crops. At harvest time, their lives were very dependent on how much they received for those crops. After their cotton was ginned and baled, it was ready for sale. Since the nearest competitor was 18 miles away, and that was a long way by mule and wagon, the farmers were more or less captive to the Harrells. So, when my father gave me the responsibility of grading and buying cotton for him, he was placing an awesome responsibility in the hand of an 11-year-old.

Let me add, I knew cotton. My father spent years teaching me. When I "cut" a bale, pulled out a wad—looked at, smelled and tasted the sample—I knew the grade, and grade determined price. I'll never forget the first farmer I faced: I did my thing and marked the grade on his ticket. He looked at me, shook his head and called my father over and said, "Elias, Wilson is too damn young to be grading my cotton; I've worked too hard to have an 11-year-old boy decide what I'll live on next year." My father, unlike me, was a silent man. He didn't talk a lot. He answered, "His grade stands," and walked away. Over the next years, I graded a lot of cotton. My father never publicly changed my grade.

Now when we were alone, he'd cut and check my work. If I had undergraded (paid too little), he would tell me to re-grade, go find the farmer, tell him I'd made a mistake and pay him the difference. That wasn't quite as bad as telling me to commit suicide, but it was close. If I had overgraded and paid too much, he wouldn't say a word—just look at me. Which was a heap worse than a world-class chewing.

I'm not sure my father knew anything about entrepreneurship, but he understood an awful lot about making a man out of a boy by giving me responsibility and then backing my hand. Since I got paid a small percentage of profits, I learned that, in the end, "fairness" builds a business; that the willingness to admit and correct mistakes is a sure way to bring customers back. I also learned that integrity is not a legal document, but a way of life. Over the years, my most valuable possession became my reputation. How could I have been anything but an entrepreneur?

# Build leaders

What about you? Are you building a "leader" or a "follower"? Are you seeking ways to put your sons and daughters into business? If you are passing out allowances, stop it. Start a "joint venture" instead. If you need help, I have a suggestion: There is a company in Coral Gables, Florida, called "Business Kids," (800-282-KIDS) that sells kits designed to help young people start and run all kinds of business ventures. I'm proud to be on their board, along with Art Linkletter and a lot of other dedicated people who believe that entrepreneurship begins at home.

## Summary

There is only one place in America that entrepreneurship is taught—that's at home by mothers and fathers. Don't let your kid grow up without instilling them with an entrepreneurial spirit.

## Lesson

From a very early age, go into business with your children. Don't give allowances—make joint ventures instead. Turn every chore into a business. Breed entrepreneurs.

# Uncle Sam
# and You

# Chapter 35

# Set Us Free

It is outrageous that almost every human being in the country can find a way to get his or her hands into the pockets of Uncle Sam, with one single and sole exception: the American entrepreneur running a fast-growing, successful company. It makes my blood boil to think that the very same people who are creating most of the new jobs in our country are being totally ignored by state and national governments. When it comes to "passing the gravy," we're at the tail end of a mighty long table, just behind the homeless. Of course it would be great if government ignored us altogether, but that's not the way it works. Oh no! They're sure to remember us, anytime they need money to pass out to everyone else.

Every time I pick up a paper I want to scream when I read the latest plan to tax and/or regulate entrepreneurs out of business. And I'm not just talking about Washington. The same sick policies are in every village, city, county and state. What the lobbyists and their elected buddies can't pilfer away from us directly, the bureaucracies that they create take indirectly by forcing us to employ more *lawyers*, more *accountants* and *consultants*, just to fill out the millions of forms some idiot has created so he or she can keep a job. What a nightmare!

## Shame on them

I recently read an article reporting that our state legislature had just voted to increase the amount to be paid under workmen's compensation. I can see all the participants in the crowd that put that little item into law: politicians, lobbyists, labor, administrators and, of course, lawyers. But, as sure as a boll weevil eats cotton, there's one empty chair—where the entrepreneur, the "bill-payer," should sit.

How will entrepreneurs pay? Taxes, of course. But worse, we will pay by not growing our companies as fast, not creating as many jobs, not buying as many computers or telephones or new cars.

Was the raise in workmen's compensation fair? Heck, I don't know. I'm just thoroughly disgusted that we were not invited to the party. Just think of the thousands of parties like that, going on around America, that entrepreneurs never get invited to attend.

I don't think any of us mind paying our fair share, but we deserve fairness. In the last decade, we have given, I mean *given*, some foreign countries enough money to pay off all the bank loans for every entrepreneur in the country. If we could guarantee loans for our fast-growing companies, we could end our unemployment problem and, overnight, get our country back where it was before Corporate America decided to downsize us into a recession.

## We're outcast

The sad thing is that most politicians think that their Small Business Administration is *helping* entrepreneurs. I beg to differ. As I talk to groups around the country, I ask, "How many of you have ever been able to get a loan via the Small Business Administration?" Normally, no hands go up. But recently, a man stood up and said, "I've tried and tried, but I have a severe personal problem that disqualifies me." "What's that?" I asked. He unloaded: "Well, I'm white. I am heterosexual. I don't use a wheelchair. I am a male. I live at home with my wife and children. I work hard, run a successful company that's growing like the devil. I haven't downsized. I have not filed for Chapter 11. In other words, I am an outcast." With that, he sat down.

The audience broke up, so did I. But what a sobering thought. What an indictment. Maybe it's right that the SBA address "social" problems. But somewhere, in the muddy water of government, somebody should start looking at ways to help the people who are creating most of the jobs.

## Shame on us

But who's responsible? You, me and our brothers and sisters all over America. Since our average work week is 70 to 80 hours, we don't have time to join organizations. We sure don't have time to get involved in politics. We just keep our heads down, work our hearts out, create jobs, expand the economy and get ignored. Right? Right!

Well it is *not* right. It's not right for you, it's not right for your children and their children. It's not even right for our government, or all the people who are goofing it up. And let me tell you something, my friend: If you think it's all going away, you are dead wrong. Just the opposite. It will get worse. If you keep letting uninformed politicians plan your life and your future; then we are all going to pay a terrible price.

## Summary

Entrepreneurs are outcasts when it comes to getting financial assistance from government at any level. What a difference it would make to our economy if entrepreneurs could get loans guaranteed!

## Lesson

Entrepreneurs are too busy building their companies to get politically active—and they're paying the price.

# Chapter 36

# How to Create a 'Boom'

If our politicians would like to create the greatest "boom" in history, they can do it in a heartbeat. Within six months, this country could be off and running, like no other time in our history. Just set entrepreneurs free.

## In review

But first, let's review the bidding. Let's look once more at what caused the Recession. The answer is simple: The growing companies of America were forced to stop growing. Our government, in its wisdom, put a killing damper on the entrepreneurial movement in this country and, thereby, brought job creation to a screeching halt. When Congress passed the tax bill that practically eliminated capital gain, it immediately dried up the principal source of capital for entrepreneurs. Entrepreneurs were suddenly forced to compete, head on, with all the

171

other "safer" investment opportunities. When Congress passed legislation to close the loopholes for Wall Street high-flyers and real estate gluttons, it threw the baby out with the wash.

If that wasn't enough, politicians and their "special interests" passed laws that allowed the savings banks of America to become the world's great Satan. Greed was legalized. LBOs and outlandish real estate deals became the financial "slop troughs" that the crooked elite fed from.

Who paid? Well, of course the taxpayers. But they weren't the only ones. The entrepreneurs paid an even higher price, because the "corrective actions" that were initiated funneled down to all banks, particularly small, independent banks—the source of most small business loans. Suddenly, entrepreneurs couldn't borrow squat. Even worse, perfectly good loans were "qualified" and/or "called" by insensitive bankers trying to please regulators who couldn't even *spell* entrepreneur. The combination of those two acts had a devastating impact on growing companies. A horror story. Thousands of entrepreneurs had to stop growing or close down. People were fired. Jobs that could have been, never saw the light of day.

All this was compounded by downsizing in the large company sector. Not only did they eliminate millions of jobs, but as a part of their belt-tightening, they also restricted credit. Again, entrepreneurs suffered, because growing companies have always used suppliers and their credit as a source of funds to grow on. New jobs was the price America paid.

Finally, there's the "gang" of regulatory agencies that seem determined to drive entrepreneurs out of business. Stupid bureaucratic monsters created endless reports and restrictions that rob growing companies of the funds they need to grow on. Money that could have been creating jobs was spent on lawyers and accountants—to say nothing about crooked payments for workman's compensation and health care robbers. Contracts were lost to minority set-asides. And whether we admit it or not, quota hiring is a fact of life. On and on it goes. More jobs lost. More new jobs *not* created.

If *jobs* is what this downturn is all about, can anyone seriously question the real cause of the Recession? Well, not unless they are blind and don't remember history. Let's not forget the 17 million-plus jobs created in the '80s. What was different then? Well, for one thing, there was Ronald Reagan. I don't know what else history will have to say about him, but one thing for sure: He released the entrepreneurial spirit in this country. And, this recession will not end until our government wakes up and sets it free again.

Which brings me to how to create a boom:

First, create a new bureaucracy. (I have never uttered those words before.) Let it be equal to, but separate from, the Small Business Administration and all its social problems. Establish a "Business Enterprise Administration" with two objectives: to guarantee bank loans for established, proven, growing companies run by successful entrepreneurs with track records for creating jobs. The size of the company should not be a factor, so long as it is creating jobs and is unable to get normal financing because it has outgrown its capital base. We could take a tiny pittance of what we spend on defense, welfare, foreign aid, tobacco farmers, college loans or "pork barrel" for politicians and guarantee loans that would immediately create millions of new jobs.

Then, we need to eliminate or substantially reduce the tax on long-term gain for investors who are willing to take risks along with entrepreneurs. If anyone on the face of the earth deserves a tax break, it is someone who is financing job creation.

The next step is to simplify the requirements and shorten the time for small companies to go public. The present SEC requirements were designed for very large companies that could afford batches of lawyers. Small companies can't. Nor can they wait around for six to 12 months, while SEC lawyers have a field day.

And finally we need to set up a special commission composed entirely of entrepreneurs to study how to simplify corporate reporting for small and growing companies, along with eliminating abuse and unnecessary restrictions. Then listen to their recommendations and *do something*.

## Boom boom

Can you imagine what would happen to our economy? Millions of jobs would be created. This country would start on a roll that would boggle the minds of economists. Our gross national product would reach heights never before envisioned. Exports would soar. We may even, in time, balance the budget. Instead of crying about how bad off we are, we could start being proud again to be Americans. *Freedom,* the other word for entrepreneurship, would take on a whole new dimension.

Well, that's the way I see it. An entrepreneurial solution. Not complicated, not even expensive. It's nonpolitical and nonpartisan. If by some magic, the president and Congress could get together and implement those simple acts, the *boom* would begin. No more recessions.

## Summary

If our government would take four steps, they could create the greatest "boom" in our history:

1. Create the "Business Enterprise Administration" to guarantee loans for fast-growing companies, regardless of size.
2. Eliminate or substantially reduce the tax on long-term gain for investments in entrepreneurial companies.
3. Simplify requirements for going public.
4. Set up a special commission composed entirely of entrepreneurs, and listen to their recommendations.

## Lesson

When a damper is put on entrepreneurs, a recession will occur. To create a boom, set entrepreneurs free.

# Chapter 37

# A Call to Arms

As an entrepreneur, I am sick and tired of being ignored by politicians. Every time I pick up a paper or turn on the TV, all I ever hear is some candidate rambling on about all the great things he or she is going to do for America. I hear a lot about saving babies, freeing women, rescuing Russia, saving the cities, improving welfare, cleaning out Congress, taxing the rich, even balancing the budget. What I never hear is anything about helping entrepreneurs.

It's time that politicians, along with all the rest of the "special interests," face the indisputable fact that the ignored entrepreneurs are America's only hope. If we don't start creating jobs, all those lofty, or not so lofty, programs to save America are down the drain. When, oh when, will they realize that for the past decade, the entrepreneurs running their fast-growing companies have created all the new jobs that made up for most of the downsizing of large companies? If the body politic doesn't start doing something to help us keep growing our companies, then America will end up sucking wind. If they keep taxing and regulating us out of business, where on earth is the money coming from to do all the "great" things they keep spouting off about? If the whole scenario doesn't make your skin crawl, stop reading.

Of course, we have only ourselves to blame. We live in utter seclusion. We don't take time to get involved. We're too busy building our companies. So, it's no wonder we're ignored. It's time we did something about it. And some of us are trying. How about *you*?

## There is an answer

The Council of Growing Companies, of which I was founder and national chairman, was formed while I was at *Inc.* for the express purpose of bringing the entrepreneurs of America together to give us a voice. We now have chapters in 23 states, with more planned. Membership is strictly limited to entrepreneurs—CEOs who run growing companies. The general guidelines for membership are two years in business, $3 million in volume or more than 25 employees. Dues are up to local chapters normally zero for first year, less than $500 thereafter. Each chapter determines its own membership. The Council is not about money or famous speakers. What we *are* about is networking and helping each other with everything from capital formation to international expansion. We learn from each other because nobody else knows what we go through. We can and should be the most powerful organization in the country. If only we will come together.

I realize that many of you may not presently qualify for membership in the Council, but let me urge you to apply anyway. Each chapter determines its membership, and exceptions are regularly made. The qualifications were not established to exclude any entre-preneurs. We simply wanted a membership of CEOs with similar mindsets and shared experiences.

The Council, which incidentally was originally named The *Inc.* Council of Growing Companies, has come a long way in the last few years because a lot of dedicated entrepreneurs around the country have said, "enough!" The Council is "owned" by its members, run by its national board of directors, which is composed of state chairpersons. From the beginning, we have had a lot of financial and administrative help from our national sponsors, IBM and Price Waterhouse.

We also decided to use our incredible buying power to attract strategic partners, who agree to pass on savings and special programs to our member companies. AT&T, Hertz, AMEX, Smith-Barney-Shearson and Hyatt are already aboard.

## Take the challenge

The mission of the Council is:

*To share the passion and challenges of growing a company with fellow leaders by providing value to each other through education, support for common concerns and greater public awareness of our collective contributions to the U.S. economy, in order to become the voice of the entrepreneurial movement.*

If that statement means to you what it does to me and the thousands of other entrepreneurs in our nation, you are most cordially invited to unsheathe your entrepreneurial sword, and come join your brothers and sisters in our "Grand Crusade."

The easy way to get involved is to fax me at 404-889-4030. I know how busy you are. I know you are besieged to join everything. But take my word, The Council of Growing Companies is different. We are *you*. And *you* are what America is all about.

## Summary

It's time for entrepreneurs to come together. It's time we had a voice in this nation. The Council of Growing Companies was formed for exactly that purpose, along with sharing ideas and getting to know each other.

## Lesson

It's time for entrepreneurs to get off their haunches and join organizations that are politically active. It's imperative that our voices be heard.

# Chapter 38

# An Open Letter to the President

Dear Mr. President,

We have never met... nor are we likely to. Since I am not a politician, or a large contributor and don't wear alligator shoes, I presume this letter will be trashed by your protectors. That's sad, because I bring you a message from the most important—and certainly the most ignored—constituency in this land: the American Entrepreneur. Wait! Don't hang up. I'm not talking about "small business." I know you think they're the same, but hear me out.

There are only about 1 million entrepreneurs—out of 20 million companies—that run *fast-growing companies*. Some are small, some large, but amazingly, the incredible men and women who run these companies share a mindset that is totally different from small-company operators or large-company executives. Size is irrelevant. Accomplishments are not. You see, this relatively small group of

# For Entrepreneurs Only

American entrepreneurs has created about 90 percent of all the new jobs during the past two decades.

Yet you, sir, along with your predecessors, as well as bankers, politicians and economists, keep on lumping them together. If all of you don't wake up and realize that these entrepreneurs are different, in every respect, from the owner of a pizza parlor, this country will continue to stifle entrepreneurial growth, and that, Mr. President, means fewer and fewer job creations—more and worse recessions and, in the end, an economic death spiral.

When selling your budget, you said that only 4 percent of businesses would be affected. Of course you are right. But isn't that the same 4 percent that has been creating jobs? Of course it is. Did any of your staff analyze the economic growth of those companies? Did anyone tell you that those were the same companies that are buying almost one-half of the business products and services? I doubt it. What will happen when you tax money away from those companies and the entrepreneurs who own them? Won't they hire fewer people? Buy fewer computers and cars? Open fewer new branches? Slow down their expansion into foreign markets?

The answer from every entrepreneur I've talked to is a resounding *yes*. With less profits and fewer employed to tax, won't tax revenues go down? Won't unemployment benefits go up? Won't the effect of less business purchases "trickle down" to suppliers who'll *downsize* even more? Where does it all end? Will you not, two years from now, be back asking for more tax dollars? Won't you again be telling America that the rich must bear their fair share? Can't you see the "death spiral" that's doomed every country that ever tried to divide the wealth? Didn't Russia try that, and England and Sweden? Is that the path you truly want to take America down?

In the final analysis, the large companies will not be seriously affected by your budget. Nor will small company operators. And, of course, the Rockefellers of this world will always find clever ways to escape taxes. No, Mr. President, whether by design or political acumen, your aim was true. You hit the only unorganized constituency in our country. And why not? We have no voice. We just keep our heads down and work like demons. And, if allowed, produce a flourishing economy.

Now that I have that off my chest, let me congratulate you on trying to *reinvent government*. Speaking for every American entrepreneur, let me assure you of our enthusiastic and total support. Again, we have always been singled out as the "burden-carriers" for all the regulators who have victimized us. Whatever you do won't be enough. Start with the Small Business Administration. See if you can persuade them that social problems should not be solved at the expense of good business loans to entrepreneurs. Workmen's compensation is a national scandal. The SEC, OSHA, FDA, IRS, EPA, etc., are all infested with uncaring bureaucrats who treat entrepreneurial companies unfairly. All the money we're forced to pay lawyers and accountants to fill out useless forms and compliance orders costs this country more jobs and economic growth than you can calculate.

While you're reinventing government, why not go all the way? Insist that Congress pass laws that will: balance the budget; give the president a line item veto; stop congressional committees from holding captive good and proper legislation; and, most importantly, establish term limitations and force legislators to come back home and live under the laws they have passed.

We praise you for the incredible job you accomplished in getting NAFTA passed, and wish you luck in controlling health costs. Let us hope and pray that when legislation is finally passed, that we entrepreneurs will not again be pre-selected as targets of special interest.

One final request, Mr. President. The Accounting Standard Practice Board is now circulating a recommended change in how stock options are to be handled for accounting purposes. When stock options are granted, the anticipated future value of those options is to be pre-determined by some formula; that amount will immediately be charged against profits and amortized over the option period. I cannot tell you how disastrous that insidious rule will be for entrepreneurs. We use options to attract the people we need to help us grow our companies. If we are forced to reduce profits every time we hire a key person, it will be devastating. We already have enough problems with bankers and the financial community as we try to raise money to grow on. This will be just another king-sized nail in our financial coffin. I implore you, don't let it happen.

Mr. President, I would be less than honest if I didn't admit that most of us did not vote for you. That's not personal; it's just that we tend to be a little right of Attila the Hun. But let me also tell you that we are fair and open-minded, with little regard for partisan politics. You have a glorious opportunity to become the kind of leader that we would follow to hell and back. On behalf of all American entrepreneurs, let me volunteer our services to work with you in any way possible. I can think of nothing that would be more productive for our country than for you to create a panel of American entrepreneurs to help guide you down the path that no president before you has traveled. Let us help you instill a spiritual revolution based on individual accomplishments into every sector of government.

In other words, let us together build a new America based on entrepreneurship which, after all, is just another word for freedom. The same freedom for which our forefathers fought and died.

Sincerely,

Wilson Harrell
Entrepreneur

# Tomorrow's Entrepreneurial Company

# Chapter 39

# Outsourcing and New Entrepreneurs

If we could close our eyes and open them again 10 years hence, we would awaken to a business world that would challenge our imagination. The large companies would have fulfilled their destinies and joined the dinosaurs. Gone would be the grand and glorious office buildings that grace our skylines today. Corporate executives would have ceased to congregate in hallowed halls of intrigue and inefficiency. *Number* of employees would no longer be a way to measure the size of a company. Entrepreneurship would have become the universal measure of business acumen.

Simply stated, Corporate America as we know it will have disintegrated, the parts dispersed into individually owned enterprises. Communication technology would have rendered distance, in geographical terms, meaningless. Home offices will mean exactly that—not only for small companies, but for corporate executives. *Outsourcing* will have become the byword for efficiency. In other words, the soldiers of the

Entrepreneurial Revolution will have won their battles. America's number-one export to the rest of the world would have become *entrepreneurship*.

It is obvious that large companies will continue to downsize. They will, more and more, be forced to concentrate their efforts on fewer core activities. "Unbundling" is destined to become a new commandment for strategic planners. Even as we speak, the relatively new phenomenon called *outsourcing* is the fastest-growing segment of the economy. For example, the National Association of Temporary Services reports that their dollar volume approached $20 billion in 1990. Think what it must be today. Imagine, if you can, what it will be tomorrow.

And temporary help is only a small part of the overall picture. Just think of the opportunities that await entrepreneurs. As a matter of fact, I believe all entrepreneurs should raise their eyes and praise our new economic savior—because as sure as Rush Limbaugh hates liberals, *outsourcing* will open the floodgates for tens of millions of new entrepreneurs to start new businesses. Never in our history has there been a period of such glorious opportunity.

For all you budding entrepreneurs out there, take heed. You can be a part of that economic explosion. So put on your thinking caps and start looking. The first thing you want to consider is what jobs will most large companies logically want to farm out? What, exactly, will they outsource? What chores are outside of their core business? Let me list a few:

| | |
|---|---|
| mailroom | janitorial |
| billing | maintenance |
| groundskeeping | engineering |
| fitness center | employee training |
| purchasing | medical services |
| administrative services | financial services |
| real estate management | marketing |

I could go on. In fact, whatever you're doing now—or want to— could become a new business opportunity. Just visit with a few other individuals who are very good at the same thing you are. Ask if they'd be interested in leaving the corporate jungle and joining you to start a new company. Be up front. Explain that you don't have any customers yet, but you want them to agree that they'll be on board if you do. You'll be surprised at how many willing participants you'll have.

When you have two or three candidates, you're in business. Hang out your entrepreneurial shingle, print up some calling cards and stationery and start looking for customers. Now, don't go quitting your job or mortgaging your home or borrowing money. Not yet. Go test the market first. Put on your selling shoes and visit a few companies—large or mid-size. Offer them such a deal that they can't say no. Which is easy since you don't have a union, you don't pay overtime or take paid vacations. Your overhead is almost zip—maybe a telephone and a desk in your basement.

What executive in America today wouldn't want you to take over all the headaches that go with employing people and living under all the stupid rules and regulations that are breaking the economic backs of all successful companies? If the first one says no, go to the next and the next—until some farsighted clever person says yes. And take my word—someone will.

Now, go back to the people who agreed to join you. Carefully pick and choose your team. Then form a company. Elect yourself president and CEO. Welcome to the world of entrepreneurship!

Just a few bits of advice: When you set up your home office, don't skimp when it comes to technology. Stay on the cutting edge of communications and information. Many entrepreneurs try to save money when they buy their first computer, software and telephone. That's stupid. Just think for a moment... when you're small, it doesn't cost much to be out in front in all areas of technology. It allows your small company to appear extremely efficient when compared to your large competitors who must incur massive expenses to change or upgrade.

Another place not to try and save money is for professional services. You may end up, like most entrepreneurs, not liking lawyers and accountants very much. But like brain surgeons, "cheap" is not what you should be looking for. Another thing: Don't be too quick to leave your basement. Overhead is easy to build, but very hard to reduce. It doesn't take a genius to figure out that there are a lot of reasons for a company to stay small. Always remember, downsizing is what got you into business in the first place. Finally, as you grow, take a lesson from your customers about outsourcing. Be sure you know exactly what your core business is, and let other entrepreneurs do those things they can do better.

If you do all this, then maybe 10 years from now, when we open our eyes...*you'll be there.*

## Summary

During the next decade as large companies downsize, outsourcing will become an enormous industry—creating tens of millions of new entrepreneurial companies. The opportunity for new entrepreneurs has never been greater as enterprising individuals start looking for ways to convert the talents and experiences into new ventures.

## Lesson

Now is the time for budding entrepreneurs to seize the day and create new enterprises to take advantage of large companies who are outsourcing.

# Chapter 40

# Women
# Entrepreneurs

The last two decades will go down in history as a glorious period for entrepreneurs. But the next decade will be remembered as the time that women entrepreneurs took their rightful place as co-leaders of the Entrepreneurial Revolution. Of course, there are already thousands and thousands of successful women entrepreneurs. Our history is already enriched by their contributions, but we haven't seen *anything* yet. There'll be an explosion of women entrepreneurs, in the next few years, that will forever change our economy, and our world.

Let's face it, women are natural entrepreneurs. They offer attributes that men don't. They're born nest-builders, excellent communicators—they know how to "read" others—and natural team players. When we entrepreneurs build our businesses, don't we try and create a "nest" atmosphere? Don't we need to communicate well with our customers and employees, creating a supportive team environment?

Women have been relegated to raising families. But that's history. During the past decade, women have been joining the work force at a rate that no economist could have possibly anticipated. The word "homemaker" is fast disappearing from our vocabulary, replaced by "working woman," "working mother" and a host of other new and better descriptions of today's world. And this is just the beginning.

Women will become the new generation of entrepreneurs because of several factors. First, in Corporate America, women are second-class citizens. They simply don't get equal treatment when promotions come along. Yes, there are laws to correct that situation, but it'll be a long time before women are truly treated equally.

But why should they wait when there is one place where equality already exists? The world of entrepreneurship. Why would intelligent, competent and ambitious women wait for some federal bureaucracy to get them promoted? Why wouldn't they say to hell with corporate culture, and go hang out their shingles and become entrepreneurs?

Want another reason why women will flock to entrepreneurship? With the introduction of "workstations," the phrase "home office" takes on new meaning. Today's women can choose to stay home, raise a family and run a business. And that's exactly what they'll do, in numbers that will defy imagination and change the world as we have known it.

## Summary

Women are natural entrepreneurs. They have all the right attributes. And in the next decade, women entrepreneurs will flourish.

## Lesson

If you're a woman who's tired of being underpaid and overlooked at work or wasting your life away at home, put on your entrepreneur hat and come join the revolution!

# Chapter 41

# Total Quality Entrepreneurship

I'm always amazed at how entrepreneurial ideas are hatched. When I think back to the exact point in time when great ideas popped into my head, I realize I was never in my office; nor was I surrounded with vice presidents...and for sure, never when consultants were trying to tell me what to do.

For example, I remember driving down an autobahn in Germany, when I pulled off the road and started shouting to the winds, "It'll work! It'll work!" Another time I was playing golf. Some of my best—and worst—ideas have come to me while I was sitting at a bar. So it was a few months ago when, at my wife's request, we had dinner with Grace Anders, who owns the Montessori school that my young son attends, and her husband. The secret reason for the meeting was for Charlene and I to hear how great our son Corbett was doing. Now that's surely not the setting for a world-class entrepreneurial idea. Right? Wrong!

Grace's husband is Dr. Theodore Dean Anders who, I quickly learned, was not a dentist or chiropractor, but a doctor of philosophy. Naturally I was impressed. I was double, double impressed when I learned that he was head of a business consulting firm that specialized in installing Total Quality Management (TQM) in large companies and government agencies. I was all ears as he began to talk about his business, using terms such as "paradigms for improvement," forming "process management teams," "team decision-making" and "statistical process control."

Of course I have read more articles and books on TQM than I can count. I have also been personally involved with companies that have spent millions to have TQM installed. I have seen incredible results. But never before had I been fortunate enough to have a real, live TQM implementor cornered in a restaurant. From cocktails through dessert, I was mesmerized as Dr. Anders gave me a lesson in TQM. It was like listening to Moses on the mountain.

About coffee time, I asked Dr. Anders—by now, Ted—a provocative question: Does it last? Does TQM remain after the consultants have left? Ted's answer: "Well, that depends." Three coffees later, I had arrived at my own conclusion: TQM is an incredible management system in theory and in application. However, it is fighting an uphill survival battle against corporate culture. I asked Ted, "When you revisit a client one or two years after you've installed TQM, is it still functioning?" Ted's answer was qualified. "It only works well in an environment where creativity and innovation can be freely expressed." I ordered another coffee.

Now it was my turn. Entrepreneur Harrell had some words to say: "Ted, TQM is fatally flawed. It is missing a necessary ingredient. You're installing a management system, without leaving behind a self-winding process. You neglect to install *entrepreneurship*, and without an entrepreneurial spirit within any organization, no successful system can endure. You can install TQM until you are blue in the face, but if you don't have individuals who are trained to take ownership, the bureaucrats will recapture lost ground and reinstall the same sick 'top-down' culture that is slowly destroying every large company in America. TQM attacks the symptoms, not the *disease*." Ted ordered a brandy.

By now, my entrepreneurial vocal cords were fully activated. I went on: "I know that TQM works, but what a world it could be if you added entrepreneurship to the process so that you ended up with 'Total Quality Entrepreneurship—*TQE*.' What if you 'branchized' every department and division of a company by convincing managers, at every level, that they and their people owned a *franchise*, with real authority? Instead of starting at the top, start at the bottom, down where the customer lives."

I went on, "Why not carefully examine how entrepreneurs run their companies while they are clobbering the hell out of giants? Why not copy their management system? Why not install what's *working* instead of what's failing?" As an example, I related the incredible success AT&T is having with their "branchizing" efforts.

By now, Ted, who had founded his company, and Grace, who had started her own Montessori school, were aggressively nodding their heads. And why not? Both had converted a dream into reality, made payroll with no money and joined the Club of Terror. They were card-carrying entrepreneurs. We closed the restaurant. But as we were leaving, Ted made a surprising statement: "You know, Wilson, Total Quality Entrepreneurship is a mind-boggling concept. It could become a product and then be marketed to companies all over the world as a new *management system*. Let's meet again and discuss how we may work together to pursue the idea."

We did meet again—and again, and again. We spent countless hours combining Ted's professional knowledge and experience with all that I have learned about entrepreneurship. What had been an idea began to take form and shape. A "product" was born; a corporation, Total Quality Entrepreneurship, Inc., was formed. Trademarks and servicemarks—to protect the name and its initials TQE—were duly applied for. As of this writing, we have presented Total Quality Entrepreneurship to two companies. Both said yes. TQE is being installed. Ted and I are hard at work preparing materials and videos that will allow TQE to be self-installed.

So, two entrepreneurs had dinner. An idea became a dream. And the dream became a product. And the product? Well, a lot has happened in the two years since this book was first published. I'll share the good news about TQE with you in Chapter 47.

## Summary

Corporate America is spending jillions of dollars installing Total Quality Management. Although TQM is a great system in theory and application, it is fighting an uphill battle to survive after the consultants have departed. What's missing is a self-winding mechanism. Dr. Ted Anders has developed a new management system that he will market under the trade name *Total Quality Entrepreneurship* or *TQE*. That system adds *entrepreneurship* to TQM.

## Lesson

Total Quality Entrepreneurship is a great new concept owned by a company with the same name. TQE may be the "next generation of management" for those companies that install it.

# Chapter 42

# Management: The Next Generation

The large, and not so large, companies of tomorrow will be run entirely differently than they are being run today. Only an idiot would think that today's management systems are working. If you look carefully at those large companies that are performing well, you'll find that most of them are coasting on something borrowed from yesterday. Things like a great brand name, or a patent or the contributions from an entrepreneurial company they have acquired. Even great companies, founded by *entrepreneurs*, end up copying the failed systems of the giants they have slaughtered. All this can change, because there is a better way. In my humble opinion, Total Quality Entrepreneurship is the answer. I believe it will replace Total Quality Management. Let me explain... but first some background.

Total Quality Management (TQM) was developed by W. Edward Deming. Its effect on Corporate America has been astounding—comparable to the Industrial Revolution. TQM has replaced "Management by

Objective" and other failed systems. When installed, it eliminates layers of managers; creates *teams* to replace individual dictators; seeks out and destroys barriers that impede the accomplishment of processes that must be performed.

It would take a book to fully describe TQM—hundreds have been written. But, for purposes of this discussion, let me say that *teams* are the basic foundation of TQM. Teams are formed at every level of management. They are composed of individuals from different levels—vertically and horizontally—who are involved in performing any process. Their jobs are to eliminate waste and duplication. The *team* meetings are open and freewheeling. Roles such as *team leader*, *time keeper*, *observer* and *reporter* are assigned and rotated. Some teams are formed and then disbanded when their mission is accomplished. Others remain in place, as operational teams. Individual initiatives become *team* initiatives. Rewards are *team* awards. Annual reviews and efficiency reports are eliminated.

I became exposed to TQM when I was publisher of *Inc.* magazine. I listened to executives of large companies singing its praises. Then I would meet with entrepreneurs and discuss TQM with them. Our conversations weren't very lengthy, because once the word *team* was uttered, the entrepreneur would end the discussion by saying something like, "There's no damn way I'm going to have my company run by a bunch of committees." Of course, I agreed, because that statement is a direct quote from the Entrepreneurial Bible—some of which I had written. Then I'd have another meeting with a big company VP and hear more astounding results of TQM. But all the time they were praising TQM, entrepreneurs were clobbering their collective asses.

After I left *Inc.* and became a consultant, I witnessed firsthand the incredible results of TQM. I was a frustrated disciple of TQM and at the same time a devout preacher of entrepreneurial management. Then Dr. Ted Anders and I had our famous dinner, and, for the first time, I began to understand that although TQM was better than what big companies had been doing, it was an imperfect system. It was missing a key ingredient: *entrepreneurship*.

When Ted and I met, I had just finished reading Roy Cammarano's book about the four entrepreneurial phases. During our development of Total Quality Entrepreneurship, we discussed these phases, and reached some pretty specific conclusions. Entrepreneurial Management works during phase one, Genius, and phase two, Benevolent Dictator, but then begins to come apart as the company gets larger and phase three, Disassociated Director, begins. In phases one and two, entrepreneurs kill giants, but then in phase three, *they* become giants, maybe baby giants—but still giants. As the organization grows, vice presidents begin to appear and professional management raises its ugly head.

But, the entrepreneur does not change. He or she keeps right on being an entrepreneur. In fact, the entrepreneur believes that the vice presidents can be converted to entrepreneurs; that they can be trained to emulate the entrepreneur's management style. "Lead with an iron fist." "Fire the weak, promote the strong." "Achieve the impossible."

You can almost hear the gems of wisdom being passed down by entrepreneurial gods: "If I ever catch you forming a committee, I'll fire you and all the members." "You don't need any consultants; my door is always open." "Whaddya mean someone wants a union? To hell with OSHA!" The entrepreneur is doing exactly what's normal for him or her. And why not? It worked. And so begins phase three, the time for grave-digging.

For Ted and me, all this added up to the fact that entrepreneurs should be left alone in the Genius phase. And, for the most part, in phase two, when they are Benevolent Dictators. But, at the beginning of phase three, when entrepreneurs begin trying to let go, they must change their management style. That's when all hell breaks loose.

That's when entrepreneurs would become logical candidates for Total Quality Entrepreneurship. Of course there will be problems because TQE cannot be installed until the entrepreneur admits that he or she isn't going to find a whole flock of entrepreneurs just waiting to become vice presidents; that there is no way to convert the mindset of a professional manager to the mindset of an entrepreneur. So, he or she must unconditionally agree that the objective is to install an entrepreneurial spirit throughout the organization. That can only be accomplished by creating *Entrepreneurial Units* at every level of the company. Every individual, at every branch, section and division of the company, must feel as though they are joint owners of the processes they perform.

With TQE, the Entrepreneurial Unit, rather than the single individual, becomes the entrepreneurial force. *Teamwork*, not individual dictators, drives the TQE system. In other words, the entrepreneur instills his or her spirit into every employee of the company, instead of trying to accomplish the impossible task of converting the mindsets, of a selected few.

In essence then, TQE is simply a management system that allows the entrepreneur to keep being an entrepreneur through all the four phases. Instead of running a company with just one entrepreneur, he or she manages an organization composed of Entrepreneurial Units, full of fire and enthusiasm.

And that, my friend, is TQE. The next generation of management. The company of tomorrow. But why not today?

## Summary

The next generation of management systems is Total Quality Entrepreneurship. A combination of Total Quality Management plus the addition of *entrepreneurship*. If an entrepreneur will install TQE in phase three, he or she can have a natural and normal trip to the Visionary Leader phase.

## Lesson

Every entrepreneur who has successfully made the transition from Genius to Benevolent Dictator should then install Total Quality Entrepreneurship as the management system directing the company.

# Chapter 43

# Tomorrow's Company

Although Total Quality Entrepreneurship is in its infancy, Dr. Ted Anders and I believe that it will become the standard for how tomorrow's company will be run. I know of no other system that will allow entrepreneurs to take their rightful position as the most qualified individuals to run large organizations. With TQE, the transition from startup to Fortune 500 will be smooth and comfortable. Just a natural business evolution.

Of course, there will be some bumps along the way. Ted and I have already discovered that the first and most difficult barrier for entrepreneurs who would install TQE is for them to accept the idea of forming teams—which they fearfully perceive as "committees."

But wait, don't all entrepreneurs believe in teams? Isn't teamwork a key ingredient to all entrepreneurial success? Of course it is. Does any entrepreneur think of his or her team as a *committee*? Absolutely not. Can't we admit that *teams* and *committees* are not necessarily the same thing?

Let me take you through a mental exercise. Go to the lowest echelons of your organization, say a branch office. Don't you want that to be a team? Why wouldn't you want two or three active players, along with their manager and supervisor, getting together to look for problems, barriers, waste, duplication and inefficiencies? We believe that TQE teams should even have a couple of customers or suppliers as members.

What if, during those meetings, they played musical chairs with everybody empowered to speak out with an equal voice on all issues? Wouldn't you like to have a bird's-eye view of that kind of meeting? Well you should, and for good reason. Ted and I believe that savings of 20 to 30 percent in overhead will result. Instead of some dictator boss telling the troops what to do, isn't it a million times better if all the players acting as a TQE team agreed on more efficient and effective ways to accomplish a process? Wouldn't that ensure *ownership*? And isn't ownership a necessary ingredient to instilling an entrepreneurial spirit?

Just imagine what it would be like to run a company composed of entrepreneurial teams at every level. Teams that *owned* the processes they had developed, with a determination to continually improve those processes? Isn't that a way to install a self-winding mechanism? Isn't that a way for an entrepreneur to get through phase three, and keep running an entrepreneurial company? You bet it is! Well, that's TQE.

Start at the bottom, where your people are interfacing with company customers. Circle that team. Give it a name. Better yet, let the team name itself. Now go up the corporate ladder. Keep going up, keep forming teams. Every one of those teams are Entrepreneurial Units, and you are going to "branchize" every one of them. In other words, start thinking of teams as *franchises*, owned by the members. You will reserve only decision-making rights for those things that a normal franchiser would retain. Can you imagine how all those team members will feel?

While I'm on the subject of team names, let me tell you that in a TQE company of tomorrow, there'll be a lot of names changed. Take "job" for example. Who wants a "job"? Isn't that where you go to be bored—looking at the clock—waiting for quitting time? Why not change "job" to "OTA," for "opportunity to achieve"? Why aren't "coach" or "inspirer" or "team leader" better titles than the hated word "manager"? Isn't Entrepreneurial Unit better than "branch?" Can you think of any word more degrading than "laborer"? Of course, we may have to change all the names back when we go visit our friendly "banker." But then, maybe we could think of a new name for him or her. The point is, corporate names carry with them generations of contempt. In a TQE company, we need to change that.

In the TQE company of tomorrow, we will use the creative talents of all our people. We will never allow ourselves to think that all great ideas come exclusively from the top—from executives, consultants, and outside agencies. That's hogwash. The most creative and productive ideas will always come from those individuals who are closest to our customers—but only if they aren't stifled by the heavy hand of corporate culture and bureaucratic dictators. Just imagine the flood of creative ideas that would be spawned, if the great unwashed were suddenly empowered to think and contribute. Don't you see? That's exactly what will happen if Entrepreneurial Units are formed at every level and then branchized.

Now let's talk about recognition for entrepreneurial achievement. Let your mind go crazy, everything from publicizing results, to promoting contests, to springing for company affairs that celebrate the "Entrepreneurial Team of the Year"—or month—for various levels. Maybe each team selects its own individual "Entrepreneur of the Year." Do everything to recognize and honor entrepreneurship. Think of the fun you'll have.

Speaking of *fun*, that's what TQE is all about. Everybody having fun. Entrepreneurs work 70 or 80 hours a week because they're having fun. They're having fun because they are growing, learning, creating, contributing, accomplishing, etc. No one in his or her right mind would ever think that an entrepreneur has a "job." In other words, if a "job" becomes *fun*, it's no longer a job. And, that's what I've been talking about. If you can embrace that simple philosophy, you're a great candidate for TQE.

## Summary

The key step in introducing TQE into a company is for the entrepreneur to accept the fact that Entrepreneurial Units or teams are not committees. Teams should be formed at every level and then treated as though they were company-owned franchises. In other words, teams should be "branchized," thereby insuring *ownership*. Only then can the entrepreneurial spirit exist throughout the company.

## Lesson

Total Quality Entrepreneurship is a powerful system for running the company of tomorrow. It involves a company-wide entrepreneurial spirit that must be implemented and nurtured by the entrepreneurial leader.

# Chapter 44

# Who Grades *Who* in Tomorrow's Company?

Once an entrepreneur accepts the fact that entrepreneurial teams are not committees, he or she is ready for the next step toward TQE—which is dealing with the question, "Who does the evaluating?" Let me quickly add, I'm not talking about "grading" for promotions or base pay or commissions—I'm just talking about incentive rewards.

First of all, let's agree that every employee has customers. That customers have needs. That needs require some tasks to be performed. And that tasks can be objectively evaluated. Now, if your employees don't have customers, identifiable customers, then they don't have jobs. And if they don't have jobs, why are you paying them?

With that in mind, let's turn the organizational chart upside down—an inverted triangle with the lowest echelon on top. In most companies, that will be the salespeople. Who are their customers? Whoever is buying the company's products or services. Where all the money comes from. Now go down the chart to the next level, say branch managers. Who are their customers? Isn't it the salespeople who work for them? Now to the next level, say area managers. Aren't their customers the branch managers? Go on down the chart—all the way to *you*. Keep asking, "Who are the customers?" Once you've got that figured out, you can ask yourself: Shouldn't customers—at every level—have the right to evaluate the product or service they are receiving from their suppliers? Think about it. Shouldn't all customers be a part of the grading or evaluating process? You bet they should!

Now, another question: Who in your organization knows most about who is—or is not—performing? For example, do you honestly believe your VP of sales knows what's really going on among a bunch of salespeople at a branch? I believe you'll agree that the individuals who know the most about who's pulling or not pulling their load are peers. In other words, the *team* knows. If given the opportunity, could they grade each other? Yes. As a matter of fact, in a TQE atmosphere, the peer pressure is 10 times greater than any dictator's threat. If you don't believe me, go ask any parent with a teenager.

Of course, when it comes to evaluating, there's always the *boss*. And it's right and proper that the boss has a voice. But, in most management systems, that's what bosses spend a lot of time doing. In many cases, that's all they do. Which brings to mind a TQE question: Do bosses have customers?

With all that in mind, let's go back to the beginning and ask—who should evaluate *who*? All three: customers, peers and bosses. Since some individuals will have more than one customer, there may be more than three. But one thing for sure, there is no way in a TQE-managed company that the boss should be the sole evaluator.

As the TQE evaluating process takes place, it will become obvious that different weights will be applied to the final evaluation. For example, the customer may deserve 50 percent or even more. In other cases, the team opinion would be more reliable and have more weight. Each company and each subset may be different. The important thing is to develop an entrepreneurial approach to the evaluating process.

Above all, get away from the idea of evaluating individuals based on their making some quota or budget. That's the failed system employed by Corporate America, as they continually worship the wrong "god." In TQE management, we evaluate based on entrepreneurial accomplishments. Profits are a natural and guaranteed byproduct of team performances. TQE means doing what's right for the company, not sacrificing the future for this quarter's commitment to Wall Street, or anybody else.

All incentive plans are complex. But TQE simplifies the process by making teams—Entrepreneurial Units—the recipient of incentive rewards, then allowing "team" members to decide how the swag should be divided. It goes back to objectively identifying *tasks*. The evaluation and incentive system is based on a simple philosophy. How well are teams performing the *task*—to answer the needs of their customers?

In determining team awards, be sure you eliminate corporate profit-sharing from your mind. By "branchizing," the sharing can be moved down. Each Entrepreneurial Unit should share in only those processes they operate. I can think of nothing more devastating and *anti-preneurial* than to "load" corporate overhead onto an Entrepreneurial Unit that has *no* control over those expenses. Remember, we do not manage by objective; we empower teams to own, manage and continually improve processes. That's TQE. That's entrepreneurship. And by everything that's right, that's the company of tomorrow.

## Summary

The question of who evaluates who is a critical step in installing Total Quality Entrepreneurship in a company. In a TQE atmosphere, the *customer's* input is vital. So is the input of the peers of the individual being graded. Of course, the bosses take part in evaluating employees at every level.

## Lesson

To determine incentive awards, let customers, peers *and* bosses take part in evaluating employees at every level.

# Chapter 45

# The Entrepreneurial Company of Tomorrow

I feel certain that I've talked to more entrepreneurs than any American—living or dead. Over and over, I've heard success stories that simply cannot be. Even more that could and should have been. But there is one entrepreneur that I predict will set new standards, will go where no other entrepreneur has been—the one who will be the first to fully install TQE. He is Leo Fernandez, a Cuban-born American who spent 15 years working for Johnson & Johnson. And though he was always a frustrated maverick, he somehow made it to management.

But that changed seven years ago when Leo hung out his entrepreneurial shingle, and started a company in Madrid. I believe Leo will go through all the entrepreneurial transitions: from Genius to

Benevolent Dictator to Disassociated Director to Visionary Leader. Instead of having to go through the painful process of converting himself from buccaneer to farmer—during phase three—he will *remain* a buccaneer and run a giant, multinational company composed of entrepreneurial teams, hundreds of them, all over the world. He will be a new kind of Visionary Leader, running the company of tomorrow—using TQE as a management system.

The name of Leo's company is TelePizza. Just 7 years old and already the largest pizza company in Europe with more than 150 stores, Leo's business is making money hand over fist and growing like the devil. And killing competitive giants as though they were lambs in a slaughterhouse. TelePizza is already in nine foreign countries. And that, I predict, is just the beginning.

My involvement with TelePizza began when Leo called me from Madrid. He reminded me that we had met earlier when I conducted a seminar at the Pizza Expo in Orlando. Leo started his conversation by saying, "Mr. Harrell, when I heard you speak, it was the first time in my life that anyone had called me anything except 'nuts'. For the first time, someone said I was normal. I want to hire you to be my adviser; because I'm about to make some important decisions, and I'd like to talk to someone who thinks like I do." After two more conversations, I was on my way to Madrid for a week. That week was followed later by another visit. Then Leo came to Atlanta for a meeting with Dr. Anders, which was followed by other TQE meetings with Leo's staff.

Leo had some decisions to make. Like an offer to sell out to a multinational company for a huge sum of money. He would remain as president. We dispensed with that decision in short order when I asked Leo the same questions I had asked myself, back when I was offered $40 million for my company: "What do you really want to do with your life?" "Are you having fun?" "Can you go back to working for somebody else?" "What will you have then that you don't have now?" "If you don't sell out, how far can you take this company?" "Can you get big enough to buy the companies that are now trying to buy you?"

Leo bounced a lot of other questions off me. I just tried to eliminate all the *anti*-preneurial thoughts from his mind, knowing he would make the right decisions. But I could hardly wait to get into his operations and find out how on earth, in just five years—with no money—he had jumped ahead of Pizza Hut, Domino's, Pizza World and a host of other competitors.

It didn't take long to see what made Leo's company tick. When we walked into the first TelePizza store, it was like attending an old-fashioned Georgia family reunion. You could feel the camaraderie that's always present when a bunch of racehorses are pulling together as a team. The excitement was contagious. Even the delivery boys, who drive mopeds 90 miles an hour through Madrid's traffic, were waving at Leo. Everybody knew him, everybody loved him. And do you know why? Because Leo was no stranger. He had spent a lot of time out there, with his troops. He knew where the soul of TelePizza lived: with his *product*, his *people* and his *customers*. Does that sound familiar? Wait, there's more.

TelePizza stores have only two full-time employees. A manager who supervises, and also puts the cheese—the most costly ingredient—on the pizzas; and the assistant manager. Together, they make sure that orders are courteously received, prepared, cooked and delivered to homes—within 30 minutes. Everybody else is a part-time worker, averaging two hours per day.

Now let me ask you a question: "Who on the face of the earth is lower on the intellectual business scale than an 18-year-old, part-time employee for a pizza parlor—working for minimum wage? Can you think of anybody more difficult to manage and motivate?"

Enter entrepreneur Leo with a creative idea. Every TelePizza store is assigned a geographical area. Every employee owns a piece of the action of every potential customer living there. Now, when an order comes in, the computer reflects a credit for the sale to each employee, telephone operators, pizza makers, delivery boys. In essence, everyone participates, benefits. Need I say more? Let your mind go crazy—as Leo's did—with creative ideas about rewards, contests, recognition, etc.

But more importantly, every one of those part-time—usually ignored, impossible-to-motivate—individuals has suddenly become an entrepreneur! They own something; their hard work is rewarded; they are free to build their business. For customers it's a windfall. Somebody cares. Somebody wants their business. For TelePizza, a breeding farm for entrepreneurs had been established—along with more volume, more profits, more new stores. For Leo? Exhilaration as only an entrepreneur can know it.

Those are examples of what Leo's doing to install TQE, to create Entrepreneurial Units. To "branchize," giving ownership, rewarding accomplishments, breeding and training entrepreneurs.

Is Leo crazy? Insane? Nuts? Well, maybe at General Motors and in all the other dinosaur's hallowed halls. But not at TelePizza. Not in the company of tomorrow.

## Summary

An example of TQE is a Spanish pizza company. The entrepreneur who runs that company has installed some creative ways to ensure that an entrepreneurial spirit is alive throughout his company. The results are astounding.

## Lesson

Total Quality Entrepreneurship works. It produces miraculous results.

# Chapter 46

# An (Almost) Final Message

Well, my friends, the time has come to draw the curtain on this phase of our time together. So many wonderful things have happened since I announced the Entrepreneurial Revolution back in 1987—not only for me personally, but for all entrepreneurs. We are winning. All over this nation, and indeed the world, entrepreneurship is becoming the accepted standard for excellence in business management. Hundreds of books on the subject have been written. New entrepreneurial organizations have been formed all over the country. The entrepreneurs of America will no longer be denied. We will be heard.

Incidentally, it has been very gratifying to see *Success* magazine become such a powerful voice for our cause. For my part, I'll keep writing and speaking—to, for and about entrepreneurs. I hope you'll be pleased to know that 10 times a year I publish "The Harrell Report," a newsletter like no other. It's a way I can keep in touch with you about current events that affect our lives. There is more specific information at the end of this book about the newsletter and about a video and an audio that I have prepared. I will, of course, continue writing my column, "Entrepreneurship," in *Success* magazine. I hope you'll continue to write and call me, particularly when you are lonely and terrified. (You can also reach me by FAX, 404-889-4030.) I have already started my next book, which in concert with Dr. Ted Anders, will be about Total Quality Entrepreneurship. I think you'll like it.

Before I go, I'd like to encourage you, once again, to take an active part in bringing together the entrepreneurs of America. Give voice to our special needs. Make America aware of our enormous contribution to the economy. Force politicians to stop legislating us out of business. I urge you to join The Council of Growing Companies; to apply for the Inc. 500 and 100, and, above all, to try and become an Entrepreneur of the Year. Join anything that attempts to bring us together.

Speaking of Entrepreneur of the Year, let me share with you a personal experience. During my time as publisher of *Inc.* magazine, I was privileged to bring that program to *Inc.* We became a national sponsor, along with Ernst & Young, who founded and breathed life into that marvelous program. We were later joined by Merrill Lynch. My involvement with Entrepreneur of the Year was one of the most gratifying experiences in my life. And lest we forget, it was the first successful effort to recognize entrepreneurs in their local communities and then make them national heroes by creating the Entrepreneurial Hall of Fame. It was but fitting that the national winner appeared on the cover of *Inc.* magazine. After I left *Inc.*, I continued to be an aggressive supporter of the program. I still am, and always will be.

In 1991, I was nominated as a candidate for Entrepreneur of the Year—for Lifetime Achievements. If I won, I would be inducted into the Entrepreneurial Hall of Fame. For me, that would be the single most important award of my lifetime. When I learned that throughout the history of the program, only one other person—Ralph Kietner, the founder of Food Lion—had ever been singled out for the category of Lifetime Achievements, I was overwhelmed with a sense of pride and humility.

The Entrepreneur of the Year banquet, at which I would receive the award, was a black tie affair for about 400 people. A few days before the event, I received a call from the program director, asking me to prepare a five-minute acceptance speech that would motivate my fellow entrepreneurs. Now anybody who knows me, knows that I can't even say "Hello" in five minutes. I slaved over what I would say to all those winners, their family and guests. When my wife, Charlene, and

I arrived at the affair, I still had no idea of what I would say. My mind was a total blank.

## What a question

Then during dinner, a friend of mine, an executive with IBM, asked me, "Wilson, was it all worth it?" I thought to myself, what a profound question! Was it all worth it? To say *yes* was not enough, to try to explain that the exhilaration of winning entrepreneurial battles was "payment in full" for all the sacrifices that come with the job; that *freedom* was a just reward for all the missed baseball games and school plays; that being my own man was fair compensation for canceled dinner dates and postponed vacations; that even my failures had been but learning experiences. I knew that nothing I could say would truly answer his question.

Then I remembered that on the way to the banquet, Charlene had turned on the tape deck and flipped it to my favorite song—Frank Sinatra singing "My Way," which, incidentally, I think should become our national anthem. Suddenly, I had an answer for my friend's question. I also knew what I wanted to say to all those entrepreneurs.

When it came time for me to be acknowledged, there was a standing ovation. I will never, never forget that moment. Words cannot describe the depth of emotions I felt as I hugged Charlene and walked to the podium. When the audience quieted, I told them of my dilemma in trying to think of something to say that would be meaningful. Then I told them about the question my friend had asked: "Was it all worth it?" I had an answer. And with the help of the lyrics from one of Old Blue Eyes' most beloved hits, I shared it with those entrepreneurs.

I've loved, I've laughed and cried
I've had my fill, my share of losing
And now the tears subside
I find it all so amusing
To think—I did all that
And may I say
Not in a shy way
Oh no, oh no not me
I did it my way.

I concluded by saying to that audience, as I now say to you, God bless each and every one of you.

# Chapter 47

# TQE—The Next Wave

The reception of TQE by CEOs has been sensational. In all my years of marketing, I have never been involved with anything that gives so much for so little.

TQE is now installed and running in all kinds of organizations. From Hawaii to Spain; from a company with 15 employees to a corporate giant with 6,000. In some cases, we have taught company executives how to self-install; in other cases, we have been asked for a "turnkey" operation. We even have our fist government agency, a division of the General Services Administration. In every single case, without exception, miracles have occurred when TQE was installed. It's amazing to see what happens when bureaucracies and brown-nosing disappear...replaced by a customer-driven entrepreneurial mentality at every level.

Perhaps the most rewarding component of TQE is the unique way incentive plans can be designed to reward individual initiatives and achievement. By allowing customers, both external and internal, to grade their bosses (suppliers), and then tie incentives into those grades, TQE immediately changes the way everybody thinks. A whole new corporate culture is born. The impact of a customer-first mentality on the company's bottom line is nothing short of astounding.

We've also learned a thing or two about the installation process. We found that everyone who hears about TQE wants it installed into their company. But then come the questions "When?" "How?" Well, the great thing TQE is that it can be installed in a matter of days. For most companies we can spend two or three days with the key executives and teach them how to install TQE throughout the company. We do that in Atlanta, or we can visit the company. There have been a number of cases in which the CEO preferred to install TQE over a period of time.

For example, with one large client, we installed "Individual Customer Evaluations" among the executives of the company, as a first step. That took just one day. Three months later, we expanded the "grading" to the manager level; six months later to all employees. Only then did we install "branchizing" and "Entrepreneurial Quality Teams." In another case, the CEO of a 25-employee company was a little skittish about changing his system, so we installed only the "grading" part of TQE. Thirty days later he asked us to come back and install the remainder. Although TQE is a total management system, each of the parts will work independently. Each producing unbelievable results. I'm so proud to be a part of TQE. I originally *thought* that TQE would be the management system of the future, now I *know* it. For any entrepreneur, TQE is an awesome weapon.

Generally speaking, there are four ways to install TQE. Let me share them with you:

1. **Come visit with us in Atlanta.** The most economical plan for installing TQE in your company is to bring your key executives to Atlanta for two days of intense training. When you leave, you'll have a full understanding of TQE and how to install it in your organization. You'll also receive all the ancillary materials you need.

2. **Let us visit you.** The most efficient and cost-effective plan to quick-start TQE in your company is for two of our TQE

experts to come and visit with you, your key executives and your department heads for four days of TQE training. We'll teach your people how to implement this customer-driven entrepreneurial management system throughout your organization. They'll learn how TQE eliminates bureaucracies and internal politicking and immediately starts cutting costs, increasing productivity and building morale.

3. **Turnkey.** If your organization is large, and especially if it has multiple locations, we'll send in a team of experts to develop and install a TQE program for you. After thoroughly studying your organization and identifying the expectations of your internal and external customers, your TQE team will develop and implement a comprehensive program throughout your company.

4. **Self-install.** If you run a small company, we'll give you detailed information on TQE and step-by-step instructions for developing and implementing your own TQE procedures. You'll also receive our operating handbook, copies of all TQE forms used by our experts and a toll-free 800 number you can call if you need further assistance.

So, my final, final words of wisdom: If you're a CEO and especially if you're an entrepreneur, you owe it to yourself to have a look at Total Quality Entrepreneurship. I promise you, you'll be glad you did.

I'll say "so long" for now. I hope our paths cross somewhere along the entrepreneurial byways. Until we meet again: "Long live the revolution."

# Index

## A

Account executives, advertising, 105
Accounting Standard Practice Board, 181
Acquiring entrepreneurs, problems with, 119
Acquisition, 117-118
Advertising, 103-108
  account executives, 105
  budget, 104
  commissions, 106
  creative people, 105-106
  importance of CEO involvement, 104
  media buying, 106
  opportunistic media buys, 107
Advertising agencies, 103

Agents, selling through, 100-102
AMEX, 177
Anders, Dr. Theodore Dean, 191ff, 195, 198, 210
Anti-preneurism, 149f
Apple Computers, 58
AT&T, 27, 76ff, 177
*Attention Deficit Disorder, A Different Perception,* 32
Attention Deficit Disorder (ADD), 34-35
  in Japan, 35
  symptoms of, 34
Attorneys, 138ff

## B

Bank loans, reevaluation of, 123
Bank mergers, 123